MW00987895

6

Strategic Writing Conferences

Smart Conversations That Move Young Writers Forward

 topics

CARL ANDERSON

DEDICATION:

This book is dedicated to Helen and Kenneth Anderson, and Harold and Marcia Epstein.

DEDICATED TO TEACHERS

firsthand
An imprint of Heinemann
361 Hanover Street
Portsmouth, NH 03801
firsthand.heinemann.com

Offices and agents throughout the world

Copyright ©2009 by Carl Anderson. All rights reserved.

Except where indicated, no part of this book may be reproduced in any form or by any electronic or mechanical means, for commercial uses, including information storage and retrieval systems, without permission in writing from the publisher, except by a reviewer, who may quote brief passages in a review.

'Dedicated to Teachers' is a trademark of Greenwood Publishing Group, Inc.

Library of Congress Cataloging-in-Publication Data

Anderson, Carl, 1960-
    Strategic writing conferences: smart conversations that move young writers forward / by Carl Anderson.
        v.   cm.
    Contents: Topics
    ISBN-13: 978-0-325-01201-8 (set)   ISBN-10: 0-325-01201-6 (set)
    ISBN-13: 978-0-325-02629-9 (v. 1)   ISBN-10: 0-325-02629-7 (v. 1)
    ISBN-13: 978-0-325-02630-5 (v. 2)   ISBN-10: 0-325-02630-0 (v. 2)
    ISBN-13: 978-0-325-02631-2 (v. 3)   ISBN-10: 0-325-02631-9 (v. 3)

    1. English language—Composition and exercises—Study and teaching (Elementary)   2. Creative writing (Elementary education)   I. Title.
    LB1576.A61594 2009
    372.62'3044—dc22

                                                        2008034944

Strategic Writing Conferences
Smart Conversations That Move Young Writers Forward
Topics
ISBN 13: 978-0-325-02629-9
ISBN 10: 0-325-02629-7

Strategic Writing Conferences
Smart Conversations That Move Young Writers Forward
ISBN 13: 978-0-325-01201-8
ISBN 10: 0-325-01201-6

Printed in the United States of America on acid-free paper
13   12   11   10   09   ML   1   2   3   4   5

Strategic Writing Conferences
Smart Conversations That Move Young Writers Forward

 topics

Contents

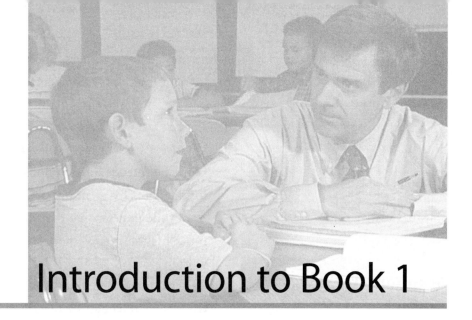

Introduction to Book 1

THE CONFERENCES IN THIS BOOK are designed to help students with the *rehearsal* stage of the writing process—the different kinds of work that writers do before drafting, which include finding, exploring, selecting, and developing a topic. Conferences for each of these kinds of rehearsal work are located in the following sections:

Part 1: Finding Topics

The student's first challenge as a writer is to find topics to write about. Ideally, he can identify topics that he knows and cares about—or that he wants to learn and then write about. The conferences in the Finding Topics section are designed to teach the student several strategies to find topics, including using topic categories, observing the world, "free writing," and identifying and mining his "writing territories"—topics that he knows and cares a lot about, and that he can imagine writing about many times across the school year.

Part 2: Exploring Topics

Often writers explore many topics in a writer's notebook before selecting one topic as the "seed" for a draft. They explore by writing a series of short entries about each topic over a period of days, weeks, even months. Typically, a student explores topics during the first week of a unit of study before she chooses one as the "seed." Then she writes the draft during the next several weeks of the study.

The conferences in the Exploring Topics section are designed to help the student explore topics in a writer's notebook. The student writes entries that will help her "try out" topics before writing in a certain genre (e.g., personal narrative, memoir, feature article, opinion/editorial, personal essay, and short fiction).

Part 3: Developing Topics

Once a student has explored several topics in his writer's notebook, he rereads his notebook entries and selects one as the "seed" for a draft. This is an important decision, since he will spend the rest of the unit writing that draft. Once the student selects the seed topic, he uses one or more strategies to develop it before starting a draft.

The conferences in the Developing Topics section are designed to teach the student strategies for choosing a "seed" and developing it. Strategies include reflecting on meaning; sketching; thinking about a story's conflict, characters, and setting; and determining the focus of and researching nonfiction. The final conferences in Book 1 help the student to make a plan for writing and create a schedule for completing the draft.

Diagnostic Guide for Book 1: *Topics*

The Diagnostic Guide is designed to help you locate a conference that addresses a student's particular area of need. The guide lists areas of need that a student may have when he's finding, exploring, selecting, and developing topics.

Part One: Finding Topics

WHAT YOU FIND	CONFERENCES THAT CAN HELP	
The student...		**Page**
… is having trouble generating ideas for notebook entries or drafts.	1. Making a List ✻	7
	2. Reading the World	12
	3. Free Writing	17
	4. Brainstorming Writing Territories ✻	22
… abandons a writing territory after writing about it only once or twice.	5. Mining a Writing Territory ✻	26
… has several favorite topics, but he's tired of writing about them.	6. Updating Writing Territories	35
… doesn't know much about a new topic he's eager to write about.	7. Turning an Unfamiliar Topic into a Writing Territory	39

Part Two: Exploring Topics

WHAT YOU FIND	CONFERENCES THAT CAN HELP	
The student...		**Page**
… has uninspired entries in his writer's notebook.	8. "Unpacking" One Moment ✻	47
	9. Visualizing and Talking	51
… is writing entries that are focused on the object or hobby rather than on the writer's experiences with it.	10. Adding Yourself ✻	54
… isn't sure how to write entries that support nonfiction writing.	11. Writing about Facts and Questions	58
… isn't sure how to write entries that support fiction writing.	12. Writing about a Character	68
… writes about topics in the same way all the time.	13. Writing in a Variety of Ways	72

A conference with an ✻ is one of Carl's Classics.

Part Three: Developing Topics

✳ finding topics

1

Finding a Topic by Making a List

WHAT YOU FIND

The student who could be helped by this conference has trouble generating ideas for notebook entries or for pieces. He may complain, "I have nothing to write about!" The writing in his notebook may:

- resemble diary entries, recording day-to-day events.
- appear randomly generated, without purpose, pattern, or depth.
- be sparse or virtually nonexistent.

CONFERENCE PURPOSE

Teach the student to generate a topic list that he can refer to whenever he is unsure what to write about.

MODEL TEXT

My list of writing topics or another writer's list

I NOTICE THAT you are not sure what to write about today. This is something every writer goes through at different times in his writing life. One strategy writers use to help them find a topic to write about is to brainstorm a list of possible topics, usually on a page in their writer's notebook. Making a topic list helps us figure out what to write about—not only on the day we make the list but also weeks and months later, or whenever we can't come up with a topic to write about.

Explain a Strategy

How do writers make a list of possible topics, especially when we are having trouble coming up with even one topic? We make a list by first thinking of categories of topics to write about. These categories may include "special people," like family and friends; "memories," or events that you will never forget; "places" that you have visited or that mean a lot to you; "activities" that you enjoy; and "issues" that you feel are important. As we think about each category, we ask ourselves, "Do I have something to write about in this category?"

When we think about a topic category, sometimes we come up with a specific, ready-to-go topic, such as, "The time my dad took me on the roller coaster at Coney Island." Other times we come up with a big topic, such as "my mom," that can give us lots of ideas for writing.

Topics I Can Write About

* the time dad showed me the newborn baby rabbits
* riding the waves at Robert Moses State Park with my sisters
* the time we went clamming in Cape Cod
* launching model rockets at Tobay Beach
* winning my first sailboat race
* when Adrian bullied me after my class beat his in a spelling bee

Share Your Writing

I want to show you my own list of topics that I brainstormed in my writer's notebook based on categories.

I started to write this list by thinking of the topic category "family." As I thought about this category, I came up with a few important experiences that I shared with my family, such as "the time my dad showed me the newborn baby rabbits" and "riding the waves at Robert Moses State Park with my sisters."

Then I thought of the topic category "places." As I thought about places that mean a lot to me, or did when I was a kid, I came up with the idea "the time we went clamming in Cape Cod." Then I continued to think of different topic categories, and brainstormed even more ideas for writing.

Coach the Student

I'd like to help you use categories to brainstorm a list of possible topics you could write about.

- Is there a category you would like to think about first? What can you write about in this category?
- What about the topic category "family"? Are there special people in your family that you would like to write about? What experiences or special moments with your family come to mind that you might write about?
- What about other topic categories—"friends," "places," "issues"?

◆ Suggest a category to the student, based on what you know about him. For example, if you know a student went fishing with her brother recently, you might say, "I'm sure you've got some good ideas in the category 'family.' What about when you went fishing with your brother this past weekend?"

Link to the Student's Writing

I'd like you to make a list of topics right now in your writer's notebook that you will draw ideas from to write about. To help you do this, I'm going to give you a list of topic categories (page 11) that you can look at as you make the list.

Remember that whenever you're stuck for a topic to write about, you can make a list of possible topics by thinking about categories. The list you make can help you find a topic to write about now and also give you topics to write about in the future.

FOLLOW-UP

▶ Later on in the year, when your class is studying a genre other than narrative, angle the conference toward that genre. For example, if the class is studying feature articles, tell students they can ask themselves, "Is there something I want to teach readers about in this category, activities and hobbies?" If the class is studying op-eds, students can ask, "Do I have opinions about something in this category, issues I feel passionate about?" If the class is studying personal essay, students can ask, "Do I have any ideas about something in this category, memories?"

▶ In a unit of study in which students choose the genre, tell students that they can ask themselves this all-inclusive set of questions: "Do I have a story in this category? Something I want to teach readers about? An opinion? Or an idea?" Angling the conference in this way helps students find ideas for writing in numerous genres.

SOURCES

I learned this strategy from Randy Bomer, who discusses giving kids a list of topic categories to write about in *Time for Meaning: Crafting Literate Lives in Middle & High School* (1995).

I developed many of the conferences in this book by learning from many educators. Lucy Calkins has written extensively about writer's notebooks in *The Art of Teaching Writing* (1994), *Living Between the Lines* (with Shelley Harwayne, 1990), and *Units of Study for Teaching Writing, Grades 3-5* (with colleagues, 2006). Randy Bomer's *Time for Meaning: Crafting Literate Lives in Middle & High School* (1995)—which inspired Conference 1— describes teaching middle and high school students to use notebooks as a rehearsal tool. Don Murray's *Write to Learn* (2004), Ralph Fletcher's *Breathing In, Breathing Out* (1996), Aimee Buckner's *Notebook Know-How: Strategies for the Writer's Notebook* (2005), Judy Davis and Sharon Hill's *The No Nonsense Guide to Teaching Writing* (2003) and Ralph Fletcher and JoAnn Portalupi's *Lessons for the Writer's Notebook* (2005) are other invaluable resources.

Topics I Can Write About

* the time dad showed me the newborn baby rabbits
* riding the waves at Robert Moses State Park with my sisters
* the time we went clamming in Cape Cod
* launching model rockets at Tobay Beach
* winning my first sailboat race
* when Adrian bullied me after my class beat his in a spelling bee

© 2009 by Carl Anderson from *Strategic Writing Conferences* (Portsmouth, NH: Heinemann). This page may be reproduced for classroom use only.

List of Topic Categories

▶ Special people, such as family and friends

▶ Memories

▶ Events

▶ Places

▶ Activities or hobbies

▶ Interesting things in the world

▶ Issues

© 2009 by Carl Anderson from *Strategic Writing Conferences* (Portsmouth, NH: Heinemann). This page may be reproduced for classroom use only.

2

Finding a Topic by Reading the World

WHAT YOU FIND

The student who could be helped by this conference has trouble generating ideas for notebook entries or for pieces. She may complain, "I have nothing to write about!" The writing in her notebook may:

- resemble diary entries, recording day-to-day events.
- appear randomly generated, without purpose, pattern, or depth.
- be sparse or virtually nonexistent.

CONFERENCE PURPOSE

Teach the student she can "read the world" (observe her surroundings closely, noting what strikes her) whenever she is unsure what to write.

MODEL TEXTS

My writer's notebook entries or another writer's notebook entries written after reading the world

I SEE THAT YOU'RE NOT SURE what to write about in your writer's notebook; that's something that happens to all writers now and then. Today, I want to teach you a strategy, called "reading the world," that you can use to find a topic when you are stuck.

When we read the world as writers, we pay attention to our surroundings—the walls of the room we are sitting in and the people around us, the windows we pass when we walk down a sidewalk, the leaves we step on when we're outside. As we observe the world, something strikes us—a dusty soccer trophy on a shelf; a crying person on a bus; a chipmunk climbing along the same path, time after time. Writers pay close attention to what catches their interest. Then they write about it.

As writers, we may notice something in the world that leads us to think of something else—a memory, a book, an overheard conversation, a wondering—and we can write about it. For example, seeing a soccer trophy on the shelf might inspire us to write about playing goalie during a championship game. Seeing a person sleeping on a bench might inspire us to write about homelessness.

Share Your Writing

I want to show you several entries in my writer's notebook that I wrote after reading the world. This one I wrote one day after spending time feeding ducks in a lake in the park near my home. Seeing the ducks reminded me of watching my dad swimming in our backyard pool with his duck, Ben.

> We spent some time feeding the ducks at the lake in Prospect Park today. There were all different kinds of ducks — including one of those big white ones with an orange beak. I couldn't help but remember Ben, the duck my dad had when I was a kid. I remember how my dad used to go swimming with Ben in our backyard pool. As my dad swam back and forth across the pool, Ben would follow, paddling furiously and quacking crazily. When my dad got out of the pool, Ben would get out, too, and stand by my dad as he was toweling off. Dad would get such a kick out of spending time with his duck — and I think Ben enjoyed the time, too!

And this entry I wrote one day after observing a lot of busy hermit crabs. My family and I were walking on a beach in Cape Cod, and we saw the hermit crabs scurrying through the shallow water. I didn't want to forget that sight—creatures so small yet so busy—so, that evening, I wrote it down in my notebook. As I wrote, I thought of questions I have about hermit crabs, and I wrote down the questions, too.

> We were at Skaket Beach today as the tide was going out, and the hermit crabs were everywhere in the water. I watched a whole bunch of them as they scurried back and forth. They never seem to rest. I wonder if they're constantly looking for food to eat? I noticed a few hermit crabs fighting with each other. Maybe one of them wanted the other's shell? Hermit crabs sure are cute, but it seems that they live a pretty perilous life.

Coach the Student

I want to help you try reading the world to come up with a topic you want to write about.

▶ What do you notice around you right now that makes you think or feel a little something extra? Take your time as you read the world.

▶ Now that you've caught yourself noting something of significance, you can write about it. That's what writers do.

Link to the Student's Writing

Here's what I'd like you to do now. Take a couple of minutes to look around the room—you can even look out the window—and see what other objects or people give you ideas you could write about in your writer's notebook. Make a list of these topics in your notebook, pick one, and start writing an entry.

Like all writers, you're going to think you have nothing to write about sometimes. Keep in mind that you can read the world anytime you want to find a topic, anywhere you happen to be—in your room, in your parent's car, on a park bench. By just looking around, you can come up with topics to write about.

MODIFICATIONS FOR NONFICTION GENRES

Later on in the school year, when students are studying a particular genre, modify this strategy to help the student generate writing she will need to write in the genre.

▶ *Personal Narrative or Memoir*

Teach the student how to read the world, looking for events in his life that could be "seeds" for pieces. For example, seeing a swimming pool might remind a student of his first swimming lesson.

▶ *Fiction*

Teach the student to read the world for character or plot ideas. For example, observing one child being mean to another might inspire a student to create a character who picks on others.

▶ *Feature Article*

Teach the student to read the world for ideas for articles. For example, seeing a child skateboarding might give a student an idea to write an article about skateboarding moves.

▶ *Op-Ed or Personal Essay*

Teach the student to read the world for opinions that could be "seeds" for op-eds or personal essays. Noticing trash on the sidewalk might lead a student to write about her opinion that people should put trash in garbage cans; seeing his mom care for a younger sister might inspire a student to write about his mom being a good parent.

SOURCES

Donald Graves writes about this strategy in *A Fresh Look at Writing* (1994).

We spent some time feeding the ducks at the lake in Prospect Park today. There were all different kinds of ducks — including one of those big white ones with an orange beak. I couldn't help but remember Ben, the duck my dad had when I was a kid. I remember how my dad used to go swimming with Ben in our backyard pool. As my dad swam back and forth across the pool, Ben would follow, paddling furiously and quacking crazily. When my dad got out of the pool, Ben would get out, too, and stand by my dad as he was toweling off. Dad would get such a kick out of spending time with his duck — and I think Ben enjoyed the time, too!

© 2009 by Carl Anderson from Strategic Writing Conferences (Portsmouth, NH: Heinemann). This page may be reproduced for classroom use only.

We were at Skaket Beach today as the tide was going out, and the hermit crabs were everywhere in the water. I watched a whole bunch of them as they scurried back and forth. They never seem to rest. I wonder if they're constantly looking for food to eat? I noticed a few hermit crabs fighting with each other. Maybe one of them wanted the other's shell? Hermit crabs sure are cute, but it seems that they live a pretty perilous life.

© 2009 by Carl Anderson from *Strategic Writing Conferences* (Portsmouth, NH: Heinemann). This page may be reproduced for classroom use only.

WHAT YOU FIND

The student who could be helped by this conference has trouble generating ideas for notebook entries or for pieces. He may complain, "I have nothing to write about!" The writing in his notebook may:

- resemble diary entries, recording day-to-day events.
- appear randomly generated, without purpose, pattern, or depth.
- be sparse or virtually nonexistent.

Finding a Topic by Free Writing

CONFERENCE PURPOSE

Teach the student to "free write" (write quickly, without a topic in mind, in a stream of consciousness) whenever he is unsure what to write.

MODEL TEXTS

My writer's notebook entries or another writer's notebook entries written after free writing

I SEE THAT YOU ARE STILL TRYING to figure out what to write about. That can be frustrating! I want to teach you a strategy you can use to find a topic—or even several topics—to help you start writing. The strategy is called "free writing."

I bet you think that you need to have a topic you want to write about before you start writing, right? Actually, writers sometimes start writing *without* having something to write about, and *as they write*, they think of topics.

Here's how free writing works: We open up our writer's notebook to a fresh page and start to write. We write about whatever comes to mind—where we are, what is going on around us, how we are feeling, memories, connections, dreams. We try to write quickly, without stopping. As we free write, ideas pop into our mind, and we write them down. The ideas don't always make sense; we might jump from one thought to another; and the writing isn't as carefully formed as a formal composition.

After free writing for five or ten minutes, we reread what we have written. Often, we find that free writing has helped us find some good ideas for writing. We can then pick one idea to write more about in a new entry—or in more free writing. Later, we might pick another idea from the free writing session to write about.

Share Your Writing

Here is some free writing that I did in my writer's notebook. I started free writing by writing about where I was—that often helps me get started.

> I'm sitting at Gate B9 of the Cincinnati airport. People are rushing to and fro all around me, rushing to make their flights. I'm pretty tired after working hard today. Really tired... I wish airports came equipped with cots for travelers to take naps on while they wait for flights... I'm looking forward to getting home. I guess I'll get home around midnight tonight... It sure is hard to be away from the kids, even for a day or two. Sometimes I think that Haskell is a new kid when I come home from a trip — three year olds seem to grow in big ways in the space of a few days, and I can see that when I get home after some trips.

I'm sitting at Gate B9 of the Cincinnati airport.

As I wrote this sentence, other things came into my mind. I noticed what was going on around me and how I was feeling—and I started writing more easily.

People are rushing to and fro all around me, rushing to make their flights. I'm pretty tired after working hard today. Really tired. . . . I wish airports came equipped with cots for travelers to take naps on while they wait for flights . . . .

Then I started thinking about what it's like for me when I travel, how I miss my children when I'm away.

I'm looking forward to getting home. I guess I'll get home around midnight tonight . . . . It sure is hard to be away from the kids, even for a day or two.

Then I started thinking about how three-year-olds grow so quickly, and I wrote that down.

Sometimes I think that Haskell is a new kid when I come home from a trip—three year olds seem to grow in big ways in the space of a few days, and I can see that when I get home after some trips.

When I finished free writing, I reread the entry and realized that I had found a topic I wanted to keep writing about: missing my children. I skipped a few lines in my notebook and started writing about it.

By free writing, starting to write without a topic in mind, I found a topic I wanted to keep writing about.

> I sure do miss the kids when I'm away. I think about them constantly when I'm on the road. But missing them helps me appreciate them more when I'm home. If they're home when I walk in the door, there's nothing more precious than the way Haskell runs into my arms, or the way that Anzia says, "Hi, dad!" in her very grown-up ten-year-old way. Or if I come home late at night, then I have the next morning to look forward to, snuggling with Haskell and reading books in my bed, and the smile on Anzia's face when she comes out of her room and sees me.

Coach the Student

I'd like you to try free writing right now so that you can see how it can give you a topic you want to write about.

▶ How do you think you want to begin—by describing what you're doing or feeling, or by describing what's going on around you?

▶ Start free writing right now! Just keep writing, don't pick up your pen at all! You can even write, "I don't know what to write" if you have to.

▶ OK, it has been two minutes. Stop writing. I want you to read what you have just written. As you read, look for interesting ideas that popped out of your head onto the page. If you don't see any yet, that's a sign to try free writing again.

Link to the Student's Writing

I'd like you to continue free writing for another few minutes. When you finish, read over what you have written and look to see what ideas popped out of your mind onto the page. Then choose a topic from your free writing and write an entry about it. Remember that whenever you're stuck for a topic to write about, you can free write to discover one—or even several—to write about.

FOLLOW-UP

Free writing is a versatile strategy to teach students to try when they are "stuck" during other stages of the writing process, too. For example, if a student is unsure of how a narrative or nonfiction draft will evolve, teach him to free write in his writer's notebook to generate possible directions. Or if a student wants to add details to her draft, teach her to free write in her notebook to brainstorm details.

SOURCES

Randy Bomer introduced me to this strategy. He writes about it in *Time for Meaning: Crafting Literate Lives in Middle & High School* (1995).

I'm sitting at Gate B9 of the Cincinnati airport. People are rushing to and fro all around me, rushing to make their flights. I'm pretty tired after working hard today. Really tired... I wish airports came equipped with cots for travelers to take naps on while they wait for flights... I'm looking forward to getting home. I guess I'll get home around midnight tonight ... It sure is hard to be away from the kids, even for a day or two. Sometimes I think that Haskell is a new kid when I come home from a trip — three year olds seem to grow in big ways in the space of a few days, and I can see that when I get home after some trips.

© 2009 by Carl Anderson from *Strategic Writing Conferences* (Portsmouth, NH: Heinemann). This page may be reproduced for classroom use only.

I sure do miss the kids when I'm away. I think about them constantly when I'm on the road. But missing them helps me appreciate them more when I'm home. If they're home when I walk in the door, there's nothing more precious than the way Haskell runs into my arms, or the way that Anzia says, "Hi, dad!" in her very grown-up ten-year-old way. Or if I come home late at night, then I have the next morning to look forward to, snuggling with Haskell and reading books in my bed, and the smile on Anzia's face when she comes out of her room and sees me.

© 2009 by Carl Anderson from *Strategic Writing Conferences* (Portsmouth, NH: Heinemann). This page may be reproduced for classroom use only.

4

Finding a Topic by Brainstorming Writing Territories

The student who could be helped by this conference has trouble generating ideas for notebook entries or for pieces. He may complain, "I have nothing to write about!" The writing in his notebook may:

- resemble diary entries, recording day-to-day events.
- appear randomly generated, without purpose, pattern, or depth.
- be sparse or virtually nonexistent.

CONFERENCE PURPOSE

Teach the student to identify and use "writing territories" (topics she is passionate about) whenever she is unsure what to write about.

MODEL TEXT

My list of writing territories or another writer's list of writing territories

◆ View this conference on *Carl on Camera: Modeling Strategic Writing Conferences* DVD.

I NOTICE YOU'RE HAVING trouble thinking of a topic to write about. Many writers have trouble thinking of topics sometimes. This is especially common for young writers, like you.

Experienced writers often have a few favorite topics that they write about again and again—we sometimes call these favorite topics "writing territories." They are the topics that are extremely important to the writer. For example, author Patricia Polacco writes again and again about her family. She writes about her brother in *My Rotten Redheaded Older Brother* and her dad in *My Ol' Man*. And I know you know more examples! "Family" is one of Polacco's writing territories.

A writing territory can be anything, and it is specific to the writer. Members of your family, a friend, or anyone important to you can be a writing territory. An activity, sport, or hobby can also be a writing territory. Some writers even write often about places that are special to them, like a country, a town, or a landscape. Writers write again and again about things in the world that fascinate them, confuse them, or that they love to learn about. And many writers write about issues that concern them, that they want to do something about.

Share Your Writing

I have a list of writing territories on the first page of my writer's notebook.

Here's how I came up with my list: I asked myself, "What topics—people, activities, places, fascinating things in the world, issues—do I want to write about again and again?"

Writing Territories

* Dad
* Anzia and Haskell
* Cape Cod
* The Beatles
* Bullying
* Global Warming

◆ Suggest writing territories to the student based on what you know about her. If a student and his brother are inseparable, for example, you could suggest the brother as a possible writing territory. Or, if you know that a student is a soccer fanatic and an avid butterfly collector, you might suggest those as potential territories.

When I thought about people who could be writing territories, I thought immediately of my dad, who was quite a character and had an impact on me when I was a boy. My two children, Anzia and Haskell, also came to mind.

When I thought about places, I thought right away of Cape Cod. My family goes to Cape Cod every summer, and there are so many things we do there that I can write about.

The Beatles have fascinated me since I was a teenager, and I can't read enough about them and their music, so they are on the list.

And there are several issues that concern me. Bullying and global warming are two of them. I want to write about them, so I added them to my list.

When I write in my writer's notebook, it's often about one of the territories on this list. If I don't know what to write about, I look back at this list. That usually makes me think of something to write about. I have written about each territory many times, and I'll write about each one many more times.

Coach the Student

To find your writing territories, ask yourself what is important to you. What are you very, very interested in? What topics do you think might be writing territories for you?

▶ Is there someone in your family that you want to write about over and over again because there's so much to think about related to that person?

▶ Is there an activity or interest you are passionate about?

▶ Is there an issue that you care deeply about that could become a territory?

Link to the Student's Writing

I'd like you to spend some more time thinking about what your writing territories are. List them in your writer's notebook as you think of them.

Whenever you're trying to decide what you want to write about in your writer's notebook, remember that many writers have favorite topics—writing territories—that they write about many times during their lives. You can use your list of writing territories to remind yourself of a topic you want to write about.

FOLLOW-UP

Some students have little trouble using a list of writing territories to generate specific ideas or topics to write about. For example, if a student writes "The Beach" on her list, it may lead her to generate narrative or fiction story ideas, such as "The Time My Dad Taught Me to Body Surf," or nonfiction topic ideas, such as "Common Shells Found on Long Island's South Shore." However, some students have trouble using their list of writing territories to think of specific topics. Use Book 1: *Topics,* Conference 5, "Finding a Topic by Mining a Writing Territory" with these students.

SOURCES

I first encountered the concept of writing territories in Nancie Atwell's *In the Middle: New Understandings About Writing, Reading, and Learning* (1998). Also, Donald Murray has a discussion of the concept in *Write to Learn* (2004).

Writing Territories

* Dad
* Anzia and Haskell
* Cape Cod
* The Beatles
* Bullying
* Global Warming

© 2009 by Carl Anderson from *Strategic Writing Conferences* (Portsmouth, NH: Heinemann). This page may be reproduced for classroom use only.

5

Finding a Topic by Mining a Writing Territory

WHAT YOU FIND

The student who could be helped by this conference:

- complains that he doesn't have anything else to write about in his writer's notebook because he has "used up" his writing territories.
- has not revisited many territories, even though he has more to say about them.

CONFERENCE PURPOSE

Teach the student to create a web to discover many ways to write about a single writing territory.

MODEL TEXT

My entry of a web of writing ideas about the same topic or another writer's web of writing ideas

◆ View this conference on *Carl on Camera: Modeling Strategic Writing Conferences* DVD.

I'M GLAD TO SEE that you have written some stories connected to your writing territories in your writer's notebook. And I can tell from your writing that these stories matter to you. This is great! I can see that you're getting frustrated, though, because you have written a story about each writing territory. You are feeling that you have run out of stories to write about, right?

Guess what? You don't have to put a writing territory aside because you have written about it once or twice. Across time— months, years, even whole lifetimes—writers write again and again about the topics that matter to them. If you looked through one of their notebooks, you would see multiple entries about each writing territory.

Writers find many, many different stories in the same territory. I bet that you have lots of stories to tell about each of your territories, not just one. I want to teach you how to "mine a writing territory." That means squeezing a lot of story ideas from just *one* writing territory. Once you learn to do this, you'll rarely be stuck for a topic to write about in your writer's notebook.

Explain a Strategy

Author Patricia Polacco has written many picture books about one of her writing territories: her family. And author Patricia MacLachlan has written several novels about one of her territories: the prairie. I bet that writers like Patricia Polacco and Patricia MacLachlan get stuck sometimes, too, like you. But we can see from their books that they find a way to write even more stories about these territories. That is because Patricia Polacco has lots of memories about her family and Patricia MacLachlan has lots of story ideas about the prairie, not just one.

One strategy we use to squeeze more stories out of a writing territory is to ask ourselves the question, "What is *one time* that I remember about this territory?" And since your writing territory is such an important topic, I'm sure you can think of more than just one time. So then we ask ourselves the follow-up question, "What is *another time* I remember about this territory?" By asking this second question, we mine the writing territory. We think of many, many story ideas about it. As we answer this question and think of ideas, we keep track of them in a web or a list.

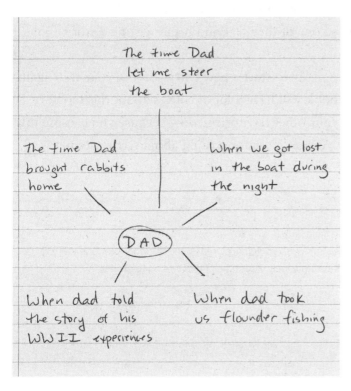

◆ It's not critical that the student makes a web to generate ideas about a topic. You might teach him to make a list instead.

Share Your Writing

I want to show you how I use this strategy in my writer's notebook. One of my writing territories is "Dad." I don't have just one memory of my dad; I have many memories. He had a big impact on me. Some of the memories are thrilling, some are touching, and some are sad. You can see that on this page, I made a web. Right in the middle of the web, I wrote "DAD." Then I asked myself, "What is *one time* I remember about my dad that I could write about?" Asking this question made me think of a time that my dad surprised my family by bringing several rabbits home. So I wrote on my web "The time Dad brought rabbits home."

But that isn't the only memory I have of my dad, so I asked myself, "What is *another* time I remember about my dad?" Asking myself this question made me think of another time with my dad—the time he let me steer his boat for the first time. So I wrote on my web, "The time Dad let me steer his boat."

I continued to ask myself the question, "What is *another* time I remember about my dad?" until I came up with five ideas for stories about my dad. I could have kept going, but after doing this brainstorming, I wanted to start writing about some of the ideas. I don't usually write about *all* the ideas that I get from a web about a topic. I might write about one or two of the ideas immediately, and then, a few days later, when I'm not sure what to write about, I look back at the web and pick an idea to write about.

Coach the Student

I want to help you mine a writing territory for story ideas.

▶ Which writing territory do you want to try this with? Let's start creating the web by writing the territory in the center of the page.

▶ What is *one time* that you remember about the territory? Let's add that to the web and continue brainstorming. What is another time you remember? And another?

Link to the Student's Writing

It's great that you came up with a couple of ideas for stories about your writing territory. I'd like you to add these ideas to your web right now and come up with more. Once you finish working on your web, choose one of the ideas and begin writing a story about it in your notebook.

When you are ready to start a new entry, look at your web again. Soon your notebook will have a lot of entries about this territory—and some of your other territories, too—because you can use this strategy to help you get ideas for writing about territories many times.

FOLLOW-UP

You may need to have follow-up conferences with some students to nudge them to use this strategy to generate story ideas about their other writing territories.

MODIFICATIONS FOR NONFICTION GENRES

▶ *Feature Article*

If students are exploring topics for writing a feature article, prompt them to ask, "What is *one thing* I know about this territory?"

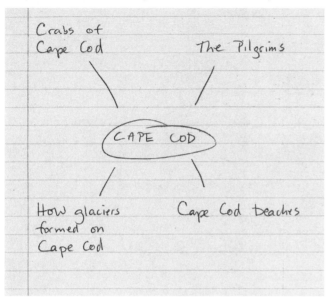

▶ *Op-Ed*

For an op-ed, prompt them to ask, "What is *one opinion* I have about this territory?"

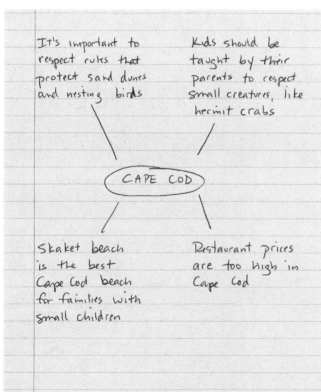

▶ *Personal Essay*

For a personal essay, students can ask, "What is *one idea* I have about this territory?"

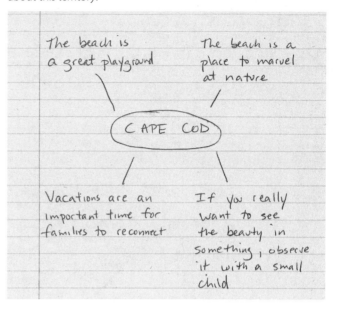

▶ *Short Story*

And, for a short story, they can ask, "What is *one story idea* I have about this territory?"

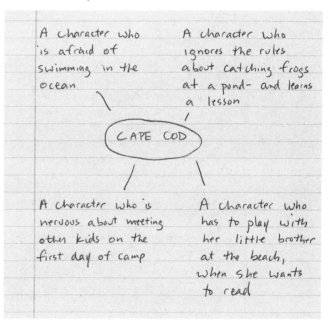

The time Dad
let me steer
the boat

The time Dad
brought rabbits
home

When we got lost
in the boat during
the night

DAD

When dad told
the story of his
WWII experiences

When dad took
us flounder fishing

© 2009 by Carl Anderson from *Strategic Writing Conferences* (Portsmouth, NH: Heinemann). This page may be reproduced for classroom use only.

© 2009 by Carl Anderson from *Strategic Writing Conferences* (Portsmouth, NH: Heinemann). This page may be reproduced for classroom use only.

Crabs of
Cape Cod

The Pilgrims

CAPE COD

How glaciers
formed on
Cape Cod

Cape Cod beaches

It's important to
respect rules that
protect sand dunes
and nesting birds

Kids should be
taught by their
parents to respect
small creatures, like
hermit crabs

CAPE COD

Skaket beach
is the best
Cape Cod beach
for families with
small children

Restaurant prices
are too high in
Cape Cod

© 2009 by Carl Anderson from *Strategic Writing Conferences* (Portsmouth, NH: Heinemann). This page may be reproduced for classroom use only.

© 2009 by Carl Anderson from *Strategic Writing Conferences* (Portsmouth, NH: Heinemann). This page may be reproduced for classroom use only.

The beach is
a great playground

The beach is a
place to marvel
at nature

CAPE COD

Vacations are an
important time for
families to reconnect

If you really
want to see
the beauty in
something, observe
it with a small
child

A character who
is afraid of
swimming in the
ocean

A character who
ignores the rules
about catching frogs
at a pond - and learns
a lesson

CAPE COD

A character who is
nervous about meeting
other kids on the
first day of camp

A character who
has to play with
her little brother
at the beach,
when she wants
to read.

© 2009 by Carl Anderson from *Strategic Writing Conferences* (Portsmouth, NH: Heinemann). This page may be reproduced for classroom use only.

6

Finding a Topic by Updating Writing Territories

WHAT YOU FIND

The student who could be helped by this conference has a list of writing territories in her writer's notebook, but she tells you she is:

- tired of writing about some of her writing territories.
- having trouble getting started with her writing on some days.
- "out of topics" and wishes she had some other topics to write about.

CONFERENCE PURPOSE

Teach the student to review and update her writing territories to reflect the changes in her life in order to give more energy and passion to her writing.

MODEL TEXT

My list of writing territories or another writer's list of writing territories

◆ The beginning of the school year, when launching a writing workshop, is a great time to have this conference with students who have learned to use writing territories in previous years. Just as New Year's Day inspires us to look back at the past year and consider the year to come, the first few weeks of writing workshop are a time when students can look back at who they have been as writers and look forward to the kind of writers they want to become. Having students consider which topics they have been writing about and new topics they may want to write about is a way to inspire them. You can also have this conference midyear, with students who need to find new energy for writing.

LET'S TALK ABOUT your writing territories. Even though on your list you have topics that matter a lot to you and that you have enjoyed writing about, I can tell you aren't so excited about writing about them lately. This sometimes happens in a writer's life.

I want to teach you how to add interesting new ideas to your list of writing territories. Why do we as writers revise our writing territories list? Many writers find that our list of writing territories evolves as we grow older. We may lose interest in some of the topics on the list, so we take them off.

And, as we grow and our lives change, we discover new topics that interest us. We may develop a new hobby and want to write about it. Our life may change in some way—we may move to a new state or our family may grow or change—and we may want to write about the change. Or we may become concerned about a new issue. As writers, when we discover a new interest, we add it to our list of writing territories.

Updating the list of writing territories usually gives us new energy for writing. We can channel the excitement we feel for a new topic into our writing.

Share Your Writing

Let's look at my list of writing territories, for example.

One of the territories on my list, "Dad," has been on my list since I was a teenager. So has "The Beatles." They have been one of my topics since way back then, too—over thirty years!

Some of the territories that used to be on my list are no longer on it. Sailing, for example, used to be something I wrote about a lot, but

Writing Territories

* Dad
* Anzia and Haskell
* Cape Cod
* The Beatles
* Bullying
* Global Warming

◆ Show the student your own list of writing territories. Be ready to talk about the history of your territories—which ones have been on your list for a long while and which ones you've added more recently.

◆ If you know the student has a new interest (e.g., recently started playing soccer) or that there has been a change in his life (e.g., mom just had twins), suggest it as a potential new territory.

since I don't sail much anymore, and the topic isn't as interesting to me as it used to be, I took it off my list.

I've also added territories to my list much later in my life. When my daughter, Anzia, was born ten years ago, I wanted to write about her a lot, so I added her to my list. The same thing happened when my son, Haskell, was born. And, ever since my family started going every summer to Cape Cod eleven years ago, I've wanted to write about it as a very special place, so I added Cape Cod to my list.

Every now and again, I go back to my list of writing territories and revise it. I ask myself, "Are there any new topics that I want to add?" and "Are there any topics that I want to retire?" By doing this, I make sure that I always have a few topics that I'm passionate about, that I'm itching to write about. When I add a new "territory" to my list, it gives me new energy as a writer.

Explain a Strategy

Here's how you can review and update your writing territories. Reread the list of territories in your writer's notebook and decide if you have been including any territory out of habit, even though you are not really interested in the topic anymore. If there is a territory you know you won't write about again, cross it off your list.

Next, think about new things going on in your life. Could any of them be a writing territory? If so, and you think you might write about it some day, add it to your list.

Coach the Student

Think about whether you need to revise your list of writing territories to include topics that you really want to write about.

▶ First, reread your list. Are there any territories that you aren't excited about anymore? Cross them off your list. Remember, a writing territory is a topic you *really* want to write about, again and again.

▶ Is there anything new happening in your life that you might not have considered as a writing territory—a change in your family, such as a new sibling, or a new hobby or interest? Add it to your list.

Link to the Student's Writing

I'd like you to think hard about your list of writing territories now and possibly revise it. You know how important the list is; you've gotten a lot of your ideas for writing from it. Remember that every now and then, writers review their list of writing territories and update it. That way, they always have topics they're excited to write about.

FOLLOW-UP

During the school year, periodically ask the student if he has revised his list of writing territories. By asking, you reinforce the idea that writers occasionally review and update their list of territories. Also prompt the student to visit his territories when you learn of a change in his life (e.g., when a student has a new puppy at home or takes up a new sport).

Writing Territories

* Dad
* Anzia and Haskell
* Cape Cod
* The Beatles
* Bullying
* Global Warming

© 2009 by Carl Anderson from *Strategic Writing Conferences* (Portsmouth, NH: Heinemann). This page may be reproduced for classroom use only.

7

Turning an Unfamiliar Topic into a Writing Territory

WHAT YOU FIND

The student who could be helped by this conference is eager to write about a new topic that she is curious about but does not:

- have much direct, personal experience with the topic.
- know much about the topic.

CONFERENCE PURPOSE

Teach the student to gather information in order to write about a topic that is outside of her direct, personal experience.

MODEL TEXT

My list of writing territories or another writer's list of writing territories that includes topics that are not based on personal experience

I THINK IT'S MARVELOUS that you're interested in writing about a topic that is outside of your life experience. Many writers turn a topic that they have no direct, personal experience with into a writing territory. For example, a historian who writes about ancient Greece can't experience the civilization that existed three thousand years ago, but she can still write with passion and knowledge about the subject.

Do you know how writers make their writing about such a topic rich and full of life and detail? Through research. Once we have researched a topic, it can become a writing territory that we can write about again and again.

To turn a topic into a writing territory, we need a plan for researching it and gathering information about it. This is the strategy that I am going to teach you today.

So how do we learn enough about an unfamiliar topic to turn it into a writing territory? There are lots of ways! We can read about the topic—in books, magazines, and newspapers. We can visit websites that people who are passionate about the topic have created to share their knowledge about it. We can talk with people who are experts on the topic, or who have some experience with it. We might even be able to attend presentations and visit museum exhibits devoted to the topic. There are many ways to learn about something outside of our experience—these are just a few of them.

```
Writing Territories

 * Dad
 * Anzia and Haskell
 * Cape Cod
 * The Beatles
 * Bullying
 * Global Warming
```

Share Your Writing

I didn't know much about some of my writing territories at first.

For example, one of my territories is "The Beatles." When the Beatles were a group, I was barely aware that they existed—I was just three when their song, "I Want to Hold Your Hand," was first played on the radio. Still, over the years, I've learned a great deal about the Beatles. I have listened to all of their music. I have read most of the major books written about them. I have watched videos about them. I have gone to special Beatle conventions and heard people who knew them share their experiences. And I have had long conversations with other fans who know a lot about them. All that research has helped me write about the Beatles with knowledge and confidence. Now I find I have opinions about them; I have things to say about their work. Even when I'm not writing primarily about the Beatles, my knowledge of that topic spills over into my writing—I find myself making analogies based on my knowledge of them, and drawing examples from their work to illustrate points.

Explain a Strategy

To turn a topic that is not part of your life experience into a territory that you can write about, you need to do some research. In your writer's notebook, make a list of some of the ways you can explore the topic over the next few months. We'll call this your research plan. To help you imagine what you could include in your research plan, I'm going to give you a list of some ways you can learn about a topic (page 43).

Once you make your own research plan, it's up to you to start learning as much as you can about the topic. Along the way, you will write entries in your writer's notebook about the things you learn, the questions that come to mind, the opinions you form, and the connections you make.

Coach the Student

I'd like to help you begin to imagine your research plan before you go off on your own to create it. Take a minute to read through the list of ways to research a topic, and ask yourself which ones could help you get to know your topic.

◗ First, what topic are you planning to explore?

◗ Wow, that's an interesting topic! Which ways of researching the topic make the most sense for you to try?

◗ What other kinds of research will you try in order to get to know this topic and turn it into a territory?

◗ What will you do first? How will writing follow that research?

Link to the Student's Writing

Now it's time for you to write a research plan for your topic. I will ask you how your research is going over the next few weeks. I'm looking forward to hearing about what you're learning and to reading some of your writing about the topic in your writer's notebook.

Remember that writers often write about topics that are out of their life experience. By researching a topic in many ways, they get to know it well enough to write about it with passion and confidence. Sometimes writers grow such an interest in a topic that it becomes a writing territory.

◆ Suggest ways students can get to know the topic. You might suggest that they talk with a colleague at your school who is an expert or that they visit an exhibit at a local library or museum.

FOLLOW-UP

In subsequent conferences, ask the student how her research is going. Once she has done some research on the topic, nudge her to write down her thinking and what she has discovered. If she is fascinated by the topic, make sure she writes about why it fascinates her. If she is curious, make sure she is reflecting on her own questions and the mysteries she finds. Later—maybe even several months later—nudge the student to consider writing a piece about the topic for publication.

SOURCES

I learned to do this conference years ago when I was working with a student who was interested in the Holocaust. During the school year, she read widely about it and became knowledgeable about this challenging subject. At the end of the school year, she wrote an article about it.

Writing Territories

* Dad
* Anzia and Haskell
* Cape Cod
* The Beatles
* Bullying
* Global Warming

© 2009 by Carl Anderson from *Strategic Writing Conferences* (Portsmouth, NH: Heinemann). This page may be reproduced for classroom use only.

Ways I Can Learn about a Topic

▶ Get an overview of a topic by reading an encyclopedia entry.

▶ Read nonfiction and fiction books about a topic.

▶ Visit websites, view podcasts, and read blogs about a topic.

▶ Read magazines or "fanzines" about a topic.

▶ Watch videos about a topic.

▶ Talk to experts about a topic.

▶ Visit museums or zoos with exhibits devoted to the topic.

▶ Attend presentations or conventions on a topic.

▶ Experience the topic directly. (For example, if the topic is music, attend concerts; if the topic is baseball, attend baseball games.)

© 2009 by Carl Anderson from *Strategic Writing Conferences* (Portsmouth, NH: Heinemann). This page may be reproduced for classroom use only.

✳ exploring topics

8

Exploring a Topic by "Unpacking" One Moment

WHAT YOU FIND

The student who could be helped by this conference has written generally about topics in her writer's notebook but needs help to write more specifically. This student usually isn't confident that her topic will yield an interesting final piece, and may be unsure or unmotivated about how to develop it. In her writing, she may:

- tell about events or memories related to her topic from some distance.
- summarize stories rather than re-create them.

CONFERENCE PURPOSE

Teach the student that one way to explore a topic is to think of an important moment related to it, to focus on that moment, and "unpack" it—from beginning to end—in her writing.

MODEL TEXT

My writer's notebook entry or another writer's notebook entry that tells about one moment in detail

◆ When students write focused narrative entries in their writing notebook and pick a focused entry as a "seed" for a draft, they are more likely to write focused final pieces.

IT'S GREAT THAT you've found some topics that you are excited to write about this year. As I look through your writer's notebook, I see that you have a collection of entries in which you have written generally about topics. You are at the point now when you can take a topic and start telling the specific stories that are inside it. One way we explore a topic as writers is to choose just one part of a story about the topic and describe it exactly. We may choose one moment from a whole story and "unpack" it—vividly describe that one moment. When we write about an important moment in our writer's notebook, we gather detailed material that we can craft into powerful writing later.

Explain a Strategy

When we want to write about one important moment, we ask ourselves, "What is *one time* that I remember about this topic?" and "What *part* of this story seems important enough to focus on?" Then we write about that time, telling it exactly how it happened.

Share Your Writing

Let me tell you how this strategy has worked for me. I wanted to write about my dad, but all I had in my mind was some general thinking about him, such as "My dad was pretty fun to be around sometimes. He took me boating. He took me to the beach." Then I remembered that, to explore a topic, writers ask, "What is *one time* that I remember about my topic?" When I asked myself the question, a memory popped into my mind of a time my dad took my sisters and me on his boat to go clamming.

> I don't think I'll ever forget the first time I went clamming in the Great South Bay. My dad told my sisters and me that it would be a lot of fun, but it didn't seem like it at first. As I walked in mud up to my ankles, salt water up to my neck, all I could think of was the crabs that were probably nearby, waiting to pinch my toes. And the water was cold, and I was shivering. But when I felt something hard with my toe, I forgot about the crabs and the cold. I ducked under the water and grabbed my first clam with my fingers. I whooped with excitement when I held it up for my dad to see! Once again, I was glad — in the end — that I was part of one of my dad's goofy adventures.

Then I asked myself, "What part of the clamming story is important enough to focus on? Which moment would be interesting enough to 'unpack,' to tell exactly how it happened?" This story had a lot of parts—I remembered zooming out on the bay in the boat, my dad suddenly stopping the boat in the middle of the bay, my dad telling my sisters and me that we had to get into the water and walk around in the mud to find clams, me in water up to my neck—with mud up to my ankles—feeling for clams with my toes. As I thought about these moments, the one that seemed most important was the one of being deep in the water, clamming. I thought clamming was going to be awful, but it was thrilling! It was so unexpected! So, that's the part of the story I decided to write about.

After I wrote the story of this moment, I had a clear picture in my mind of what happened that afternoon. I felt I had relived the moment! Going back in time like this reminded me of how much fun I had with my dad on his crazy adventures, and I got excited by the possibility of taking this entry and turning it into a well-developed personal narrative to publish.

Coach the Student

I want to help you to "unpack" a moment from one part of your topic and write a story.

▶ What is *one time* that you remember especially about your topic?

▶ What *one part* of this story seems important enough to focus on? Which moment would be interesting enough to tell exactly how it happened?

Link to the Student's Writing

I love how you've thought of *one time* that you remember about your topic. I'd like you to "unpack" this moment. Write an entry about this one time right now, as a way to explore the topic. After you write the entry, try writing another, thinking again about a very important moment related to a topic.

When you write a story about a topic in your writer's notebook, try choosing one small part of the story, a part that feels very important to you, and write only about that moment. By focusing

◆ When students are having trouble deciding which part of the story is most important to "unpack," ask them to tell you all the parts of the story, from beginning to end. Then, retell those parts to them, and ask again which part is most important. It's usually easier for students to decide on a part to focus on at this point.

on one part of a story in detail, you're going to get a better sense of whether you want to go further with the story and turn it into a piece of writing to publish.

FOLLOW-UP

Some students may think of a story related to a topic, but instead of writing about one moment of the story, they may write the entire story, from beginning to end, over several pages. Ask them to write about only a couple of minutes of the story—a couple of minutes that feel especially important to them.

SOURCES

Lucy Calkins and her colleagues at the Teachers College Reading and Writing Project (TCRWP) describe the value of teaching students to write focused entries in their writer's notebooks in the book series *Units of Study for Teaching Writing, Grades 3–5* (2006).

I don't think I'll ever forget the first time I went clamming in the Great South Bay. My dad told my sisters and me that it would be a lot of fun, but it didn't seem like it at first. As I walked in mud up to my ankles, salt water up to my neck, all I could think of was the crabs that were probably nearby, waiting to pinch my toes. And the water was cold, and I was shivering. But when I felt something hard with my toe, I forgot about the crabs and the cold. I ducked under the water and grabbed my first clam with my fingers. I whooped with excitement when I held it up for my dad to see! Once again, I was glad—in the end—that I was part of one of my dad's goofy adventures.

© 2009 by Carl Anderson from *Strategic Writing Conferences* (Portsmouth, NH: Heinemann). This page may be reproduced for classroom use only.

9

Exploring a Topic by Visualizing and Talking

WHAT YOU FIND
The student who could be helped by this conference is writing entries that are very short and quite sparse.

CONFERENCE PURPOSE
Teach the student to visualize and talk about an experience in order to prepare to write with more depth and breadth.

MODEL TEXT
My writer's notebook entry or another writer's notebook entry with vivid details

◆ You don't need a baseball story like mine to have this conference. Tell a story about something you learned to do through practice (e.g., riding a bike, running several miles around a park, playing a lot of chords on a guitar) to make the same point: Over time, and with practice, we improve.

I LIKE HOW YOU CHOSE one small part of your experience to focus on for your entry. That is great! This entry is very short, though. I bet there is more than just this one sentence that you could say about this event, right?

I think who you are as a writer is a lot like who I was as a baseball player when I first started playing as a boy. Way back then, when I hit the ball, it wouldn't go very far—to the pitcher maybe, or to the second baseman if I was having a really good day. Only after I played baseball for a while was I able to hit the ball into the outfield—and, eventually, hit a home run.

As writers, we can use our notebooks to refresh our memory of an important experience and to write an entry that can become a "seed" for a vivid story. To write an entry that is going to be helpful for writing a story, we need to learn how to write longer, more detailed entries—home run entries! The longer and more detailed an entry is, the easier it is to stretch it into an even more detailed story that will "grab" our readers. To write a longer entry, we spend more time on the story, re-experiencing each part in our minds vividly. When we get a better "feel" for a story, we are more excited to write it as an entry in our writer's notebook, and we are better able to decide whether it's a good one to pick as a "seed" for a draft later on.

Explain a Strategy

A strategy that we can use to help us write with more detail is to visualize and talk out the story to a friend before we write it. As we tell the story, sometimes over and over, we remember more of the details. This happens because as we tell the story, we visualize it—we "see it" in our mind—and try to describe what we "see." As we tell the story, we keep asking ourselves, "Can I tell more about *this* part?" We ask this question because we see when our friend is really interested in a certain part of the story. To keep the friend interested, we come up with even more details. When we sit down later to write the story, we find that we have much more to write.

I'm going to demonstrate this strategy for you. I have a memory about a giant toad at the beach. The part of the story that feels important to me is when I caught the toad. I'm going to tell you that one part of the story. As I tell the story, I'm going to come up with a lot of details about what happened. First, I get a picture in my mind of what happened that afternoon. Then, I describe what I "see"—what I was doing and what the other character (the toad) was doing.

> After looking for ten or fifteen minutes, I finally spied the toad hopping through the beach reeds. I tiptoed up to it quietly, hoping it wouldn't notice me.

Right now, I'm asking myself if there is more to say about this part of the story. There is! I'm "seeing" more of what I was doing.

> I got within a few inches of the toad. Slowly, I reached my hands out to grab the toad.

I can see by the expression on your face that you're really interested in this part of the story. I'm going to try to tell this part with even more detail, because I think you would appreciate a lot of detail right now.

> And then I crept up to the toad, and I was inches from its large body. Suddenly, the toad leaped a foot, maybe more. The chase was on!

There's more to the story, but I think I've told enough of it for you to see that when I talk out the story, I come up with a lot of details. When I sit down to write about this important part of the story—catching that humongous toad—I'll be able to write it in a nicely detailed way.

By taking the time to think about the story like this, I also get more excited about it. When I write it as an entry, I'll be even more excited. I already think that this story might end up being the "seed" for a draft.

Coach the Student

Let's look over your entries and find one that we can try this "visualize and talk" strategy with. I'd like you to practice telling the story before you write it again in your notebook.

▶ As you tell the story, try to "see" it in your head, and describe what you "see." What are you doing? What are other characters doing?

▶ Great! Tell me more about that part.

▶ I'm really interested in the part you're telling right now. Could you tell me even more about it?

Link to the Student's Writing

I'd like you to practice telling this story one more time before you write it. Who in the class do you want to tell it to? After you've told the story to your classmate, you will be ready to try to write a lot about it in your writer's notebook.

Whenever you are witing a short, skimpy entry that lacks detail, you can use this strategy. Talking out a story before you write it is a great way to write longer, more detailed entries. Try visualizing and telling the story before you write other entries in your notebook, too.

FOLLOW-UP

▶ You can't be there every time your students want to talk out a story. Partner them so that they can tell their stories to each other before they write.

▶ Have this conference with students who are exploring topics for genres other than personal narrative. If students are going to write feature articles, they may talk out the facts and details about their specific topics with their writing partners before they write.

SOURCES

Donald Murray's thinking about how writers visualize their topics as they write is the inspiration for this conference. You can read more about this in *Write to Learn* (2004).

10

Exploring a Topic by Adding Yourself

WHAT YOU FIND

The student who could be helped by this conference is writing entries that are:

- focused on the object or hobby (e.g., toys, movies, video games) rather than on the student himself.
- filled with specific—but arcane—details of the object, instead of being focused on the student's experiences of doing or watching it.

CONFERENCE PURPOSE

Teach the student to write personal narratives that focus on himself or his experiences rather than on objects or hobbies.

MODEL TEXTS

My Rotten Redheaded Older Brother by Patricia Polacco or another personal narrative

My writer's notebook entry or another writer's notebook entry about an experience, rather than an object or a hobby

◆ Use this conference to improve any dull, procedural narrative, voiceless retelling, or impersonal description. In addition to video games, other topics also frequently take students away from telling stories about themselves. When students write about sports, for example, they often summarize what happened in the game and leave themselves out of the action. When you see this happening, have this same conference with them.

I can see that you know a lot of things about this video game. In fact, I'm going to write down in my notes that you are an expert on this game. Later in the year, when we study nonfiction writing, you could write a great feature article in which you teach readers what you know about this game or a wonderful review of the game.

But right now, we are writing stories in our writer's notebooks, and we will be turning these entries into personal narratives. I know that video games are really important to you, and I can tell that you are good at them. I think the video game is a great topic for an entry and that you can stretch into a personal narrative story. When I read this entry though, it feels like it is more focused on the details of the game than it is on you. And personal narrative stories are *personal*. They are about you and your experiences, not the details of the game—because it's the part about you that makes a reader want to read more.

So, I want to teach you how to bring *you* into your story about your video game. The trick is to make *you* the subject instead of the video game. Many video game stories are really stories of personal triumph ("After a lot of hard work, I got to Level 20!"), friendship ("My friend and I had a great time playing together."), or rivalry ("I beat my brother in *Space Invaders*!"). The emotions are the part of the story that draws readers in and makes them want to read more.

Explain a Strategy

When writers write a story, they focus on the people or characters who play a role in it—what the people say, do, and feel. For example, in *My Rotten Redheaded Older Brother*, when author

◆ We may cringe when we find students—often boys—writing about video games. It's hard to envision how students could possibly turn what happens in Level 14 of a game into a meaningful personal narrative. Consequently, it's common for teachers to discourage video games as a topic. However, if we discourage students from writing about topics that matter to them, they may never learn what writing can do for them. So, instead, try teaching students to write entries in which they themselves are the focus, entries that can be crafted into well-written personal narratives.

Patricia Polacco writes about challenging her brother to a rhubarb-eating contest, she doesn't just describe the rhubarb. She writes about what she said to her brother, how he reacted, and how she felt when he won the contest. These types of details—about the people in the story—are what make readers connect with the story. Details about the people are what make a story funny, exciting, touching, or sad.

Let's work on how we can start writing about *you* when you write your video game story, not just about the details of the game. Start by asking yourself, "What is *one time* that I remember playing a video game?" Once you come up with one time, the trick is to remember to write about *you* playing the game, and, if you weren't playing alone, about the other people playing with you. For example, write about what you were doing, what anybody else who was playing with you was doing, what you were saying, and what you were thinking as you were playing. If you write about these kinds of details, your entry will be a story about *you* playing the game.

Share Your Writing

Let me show you an entry that I wrote about playing a video game that will help you see what I'm talking about.

> One time, I was playing a video game with my friend Jeff. It was called Space Invaders. Usually, Jeff beat me—and he loved to talk about how much better he was than I was at the game. This made me mad. But this time was different. During my second turn, I couldn't do any wrong. I shot down every alien invader with ease, and I went from the first level to the second level and then to the third level. Jeff couldn't believe it. He kept saying, "Now you're going to get killed, I know it." I just told him, "Keep quiet!" Finally, when my turn was over, I was ahead by 20,000 points, a really big lead. Jeff wasn't able to catch up the rest of the game. I had a great time saying to Jeff that I was the Space Invaders champ!

By focusing on what I was doing and saying, and what Jeff was doing and saying, and by writing what I was thinking while we were playing, I wrote a story about playing the video game. This is the kind of entry that could make a wonderful published story, if I were to pick it as a "seed" to develop into a draft.

Coach the Student

I'd like to help you write a story about your video game by asking you some questions.

- What is *one time* that you remember playing the game?
- What part of the story feels important to write about?
- What were you *doing* in this part of the story?
- What was the person playing with you doing?
- What were you saying? What were the people you were playing with saying?
- What were you thinking during the game?

Link to the Student's Writing

I think you've got a great story about playing this video game. It's time now to write the story as an entry in your writer's notebook. Whenever you write a story in your notebook about a topic such as playing a video game, remember to make it a story about *you*.

FOLLOW-UP

- As the school year unfolds, encourage students who like to write about video games or sports games to write in other genres that may satisfy their passion for talking about details of games. Feature articles, how-to pieces, and reviews are genres in which students can often write successfully.
- Be open to students writing fiction based on their favorite video game. (There actually are writers who write novels based on popular video games, such as *Halo!*) Students could do this during a unit of study in which they can choose the genre.

SOURCES

Two books about young writers have helped me value student-picked topics, such as video games: Tom Newkirk's *Misreading Masculinity: Boys, Literacy, and Popular Culture* (2002) and Ralph Fletcher's *Boy Writers: Reclaiming Their Voices* (2006).

One time, I was playing a video game with my friend Jeff. It was called Space Invaders. Usually, Jeff beat me — and he loved to talk about how much better he was than I was at the game. This made me mad. But this time was different. During my second turn, I couldn't do any wrong. I shot down every alien invader with ease, and I went from the first level to the second level and then to the third level. Jeff couldn't believe it. He kept saying, "Now you're going to get killed, I know it." I just told him, "Keep quiet!" Finally, when my turn was over, I was ahead by 20,000 points, a really big lead. Jeff wasn't able to catch up the rest of the game. I had a great time saying to Jeff that I was the Space Invaders champ!

© 2009 by Carl Anderson from *Strategic Writing Conferences* (Portsmouth, NH: Heinemann). This page may be reproduced for classroom use only.

11

Exploring a Nonfiction Topic by Writing about Facts and Questions

WHAT YOU FIND

The student who could be helped by this conference expresses confusion about:

- how to explore a topic she is considering as a "seed" for nonfiction writing (e.g., a feature article, op-ed, or personal essay).
- how to write entries about her writing territories that support nonfiction writing.

CONFERENCE PURPOSE

Teach the student she can write about interesting facts or ask questions to explore topics she is considering as "seeds" in a nonfiction genre.

MODEL TEXTS

My writer's notebook entries or another writer's notebook entries that explore topics for nonfiction writing

◆ A *feature article* gives information about a topic to a reader. You can find examples of feature articles in *TIME For Kids*, *Highlights*, *Boys' Life*, *Ranger Rick*, and similar magazines for students.

IT'S EXCITING TO BE writing in a different genre, isn't it? There are so many interesting topics to write about in nonfiction. But sometimes it is hard to get started. I'd like to talk with you about exploring topics you are considering writing about.

Before we write nonfiction, we may explore several topics first. Developing these topics by writing stories isn't useful because the subject of nonfiction (e.g., a feature article) isn't *you*. Instead, we can explore a topic we are considering as a "seed" by writing about its interesting facts and by asking questions about it.

Share Your Writing

I want to show you two kinds of entries in my writer's notebook. In one kind of entry, I try to remember some of the interesting information I've learned about the topic. To get started writing this kind of entry, I ask myself, "What interesting facts do I know about the topic?" Sometimes as I write, I start to feel energized about the topic, which is a signal that the topic might be a good "seed" for a feature article.

Let's look at one of these entries together. In this entry, I wrote about some of the things I know about lobsters, which is an aspect of my writing territory, Cape Cod.

> The more I learn about lobsters, the more interesting they become to me! I think it's fascinating that centuries ago, lobster wasn't considered a delicacy — it was so poorly regarded, it was fed to prisoners in jails! Or that lobstermen have very specific territories that they fish — and if anyone else tries to fish there, they sometimes cut their trap lines, even have "wars" over territories! Or that the 1½ pound lobsters that we eat are about seven years old — and that the really big ones in the store, the ones that weigh ten pounds or more, are seventy or eighty years old!

You can see that I wrote down some of the interesting things I know about lobsters and lobstering. I had a lot of fun taking the time to write these things down, which made me think that this topic would be a good one to write an article about.

In another kind of entry, I wonder about a topic. I ask myself, "What questions do I have about this topic?" Then I write down the questions and my speculations about the answers. When I wonder about a topic like this, I sometimes find that my curiosity increases. I feel driven to write an article about it because writing an article gives me the opportunity to research the topic and find out answers to my questions. I tried writing about my wonderings in this entry about glaciers.

> I learned today that the fresh water "kettle" ponds that we swim in here at Cape Cod were formed when the glaciers receded, leaving big pieces behind to melt. How long ago was the last ice age? How exactly do the glaciers push earth ahead of them— the earth that eventually formed Cape Cod? If so much water was frozen, then how much lower was the sea level during the last ice age?

In this entry, I wrote about the glaciers that formed Cape Cod years and years ago. I sure have a lot of questions about the glacier, don't I? If I wrote an article about this topic, I'd get to research it and find out the answers to all of these questions.

Coach the Student

I'd like to help you explore a topic you are considering as a "seed" for a nonfiction piece.

▶ What topic do you want to write about?

▶ What interesting facts do you know about the topic?

▶ What questions do you have about this topic? What do you wonder about it?

Link to the Student's Writing

Start by writing an entry about the facts you know or the questions you have about your topic. That way, you can explore it as a possible "seed." When you are deciding on a nonfiction topic to write about, two ways you can explore the topic are to write interesting facts about it and to wonder about it.

SOURCES

I designed this conference to teach students to explore topics for nonfiction genres after I learned its value from many educators, including Randy Bomer (*Time for Meaning: Crafting Literate Lives in Middle & High School*, 1995), Randy and Katherine Bomer (*For a Better World: Reading and Writing for Social Action*, 2001), and Lucy Calkins and Cory Gillette (*Breathing Life into Essays*, 2006).

MODIFICATIONS FOR NONFICTION GENRES

▶ Op-Ed

◆ Writers write **op-eds** (opinions and editorials) to explain their position on an issue, to try to convince readers to believe as they do. You can find examples of op-eds in the editorial section of a newspaper.

◆ Say, "In one kind of entry, I try to figure out my opinion about a topic. I ask myself, 'What do I believe about this topic?' and then write my thoughts down. This helps me figure out what my opinion is." See below for an example of this kind of entry.

> Seeing a kid get picked on outside a school today got my blood boiling, as it usually does. It's so important that schools have anti-bullying initiatives to deal with the problem. Although I know that kids who bully often have serious problems themselves, I can't help but think of the damage that bullying does to kids who are the victims of it. The humiliation of the experience, and the damage to a kid's self-esteem, can last for a long, long time.

◆ Say, "In another kind of entry, I think about an opinion I already have, something I believe. To get started writing, I ask myself, 'What **exactly** is my opinion?'" See below for an example of this kind of entry.

> I'm trying to decide how I feel about video games. I can see several benefits for kids who play them. They're often intricate puzzles to figure out, so they challenge their minds. Many of them are played with other kids, so they can give kids something fun to do together. And they can be a great way to blow off steam! On the other hand, I don't like how some kids spend tons of time playing them. I guess I think video games are okay, within limits. As long as kids don't play them beyond an hour a day, then I think I can live with them, even appreciate their place in kids' lives.

▶ Personal Essay

◆ In a **personal essay**, writers explore an idea they have about a topic. You can find examples of personal essays in a magazine, such as **Newsweek** (the "My Turn" section), and in the lifestyle section of a newspaper, such as **USA Today** (the "Life" section).

◆ Say, "In one kind of entry, I try to figure out my ideas about a topic. I ask myself, 'What do I think about this topic?' and then write my thinking down. This helps me figure out what the main idea is." See below for an example of this kind of entry.

> Dads sure can be embarrassing to their kids! All I have to do is think of my own dad, singing the theme song to "The Flintstones" television show, and my face still turns red! Or think about dad's pot belly, and how it made it difficult for him to keep his bathing suit around his waist — or think about how my dad often tried to use "kid language" around me when I was with my friends, which sounded so strange coming out of the mouth of a fifty year old man!

◆ Say, "In another kind of entry, I try to explain my main idea. To get started writing this kind of entry, I ask myself, 'What **exactly** is my idea?'" See below for an example of this kind of entry.

> I sure love being a dad. Last night, when I came home from work, Haskell asked me to play "horsie." Suddenly, I found myself on all fours, with him on my back, telling me to "giddyup!" Then Haskell wanted to build a fort, so in just a few minutes, we had all the pillows off the couch and piled up around us. One of the things I love so much about being a dad is the opportunity it gives me to stop acting like an adult sometimes, and act like a kid again!

The more I learn about lobsters, the more interesting they become to me! I think it's fascinating that centuries ago, lobster wasn't considered a delicacy — it was so poorly regarded, it was fed to prisoners in jails! Or that lobstermen have very specific territories that they fish — and if anyone else tries to fish there, they sometimes cut their trap lines, even have "wars" over territories! Or that the 1½ pound lobsters that we eat are about seven years old — and that the really big ones in the store, the ones that weigh ten pounds or more, are seventy or eighty years old!

© 2009 by Carl Anderson from *Strategic Writing Conferences* (Portsmouth, NH: Heinemann). This page may be reproduced for classroom use only.

I learned today that the fresh water "kettle" ponds that we swim in here at Cape Cod were formed when the glaciers receded, leaving big pieces behind to melt. How long ago was the last ice age? How exactly do the glaciers push earth ahead of them— the earth that eventually formed Cape Cod? If so much water was frozen, then how much lower was the sea level during the last ice age?

© 2009 by Carl Anderson from *Strategic Writing Conferences* (Portsmouth, NH: Heinemann). This page may be reproduced for classroom use only.

Seeing a kid get picked on outside a school today got my blood boiling, as it usually does. It's so important that schools have anti-bullying initiatives to deal with the problem. Although I know that kids who bully often have serious problems themselves, I can't help but think of the damage that bullying does to kids who are the victims of it. The humiliation of the experience, and the damage to a kid's self-esteem, can last for a long, long time.

© 2009 by Carl Anderson from *Strategic Writing Conferences* (Portsmouth, NH: Heinemann). This page may be reproduced for classroom use only.

I'm trying to decide how I feel about video games. I can see several benefits for kids who play them. They're often intricate puzzles to figure out, so they challenge their minds. Many of them are played with other kids, so they can give kids something fun to do together. And they can be a great way to blow off steam! On the other hand, I don't like how some kids spend tons of time playing them. I guess I think video games are okay, within limits. As long as kids don't play them beyond an hour a day, then I think I can live with them, even appreciate their place in kids' lives.

© 2009 by Carl Anderson from *Strategic Writing Conferences* (Portsmouth, NH: Heinemann). This page may be reproduced for classroom use only.

Dads sure can be embarrassing to their kids! All I have to do is think of my own dad, singing the theme song to "The Flintstones" television show, and my face still turns red! Or think about dad's pot belly, and how it made it difficult for him to keep his bathing suit around his waist — or think about how my dad often tried to use "kid language" around me when I was with my friends, which sounded so strange coming out of the mouth of a fifty year old man!

© 2009 by Carl Anderson from *Strategic Writing Conferences* (Portsmouth, NH: Heinemann). This page may be reproduced for classroom use only.

I sure love being a dad. Last night, when I came home from work, Haskell asked me to play "horsie." Suddenly, I found myself on all fours, with him on my back, telling me to "giddyup!" Then Haskell wanted to build a fort, so in just a few minutes, we had all the pillows off the couch and piled up around us. One of the things I love so much about being a dad is the opportunity it gives me to stop acting like an adult sometimes, and act like a kid again!

© 2009 by Carl Anderson from *Strategic Writing Conferences* (Portsmouth, NH: Heinemann). This page may be reproduced for classroom use only.

Exploring a Fiction Topic by Writing about a Character

WHAT YOU FIND

The student who could be helped by this conference is writing fiction but is:

- writing entries that are short plot summaries or drafts of a short story.

CONFERENCE PURPOSE

Teach the student to write fiction entries about a character to prepare to write an interesting, well-developed short story.

MODEL TEXT

My writer's notebook entry or another writer's notebook entry that describes a character

I CAN SEE FROM your notebook that you have started to write a story, and I can tell you are excited to write fiction. But now that you have started writing, you're not really sure where it is going, right? I want to talk with you about how fiction writers often get started writing. This may surprise you, but fiction writers *don't* usually get started by making up the plot of their stories. Instead, they often start by creating a character in their writer's notebook. Once they know the character well, *then* they figure out a story to tell about the character.

Explain a Strategy

So, what does it mean to create a character? We can start with a basic story premise—an idea about a problem or a conflict a character has. Then, in our writer's notebook, we create a character by asking, "What kind of person would have this problem or conflict?" We might describe what the character looks like, the family and friends, where the character lives, what he or she likes to do, and even what the character doesn't like to do. And we also think a lot about the character's problem or conflict. Thinking about the problem or conflict is especially important because the plot is about how the main character deals with it. We need to know the main character's problem or conflict inside and out before we can figure out what's going to happen to the character in the story.

Sarah:

* Sarah's best friend has started to play with another girl
* Sarah is seven years old
* she lives in Park Slope, Brooklyn
* lives with mom (Julie) and dad (Keith)
* has a younger sister, Lila, who is five
* likes to play soccer, do outdoor sports
* goes to PS 321
* she's in the second grade
* her best friend's name is Anna
* they've been in the same class since kindergarten
* they usually spend recess together every day, and like to kick a soccer ball around the schoolyard.
* the girl Anna has started to play with is Jodi
* Anna and Jodi are now playing together at recess – without Sarah
* Sarah is feeling left out, and doesn't know how to handle the situation

◆ Students are eager to write fiction. In their zeal, they often plunge into writing a story without really thinking about "where they're going" with it. They come up with an interesting premise and start writing, making up the plot as they go along. The result? Very often a story with a plot that's hard to follow—and very often one that's hard to invest oneself in as a reader.

Fiction writers do a great deal of work before starting a story. Commonly, they begin by imagining a character and getting to know him—his family, where he lives, likes and dislikes, the things he does, etc. Most important, fiction writers figure out what a character *needs* to resolve a problem or conflict, such as companionship, learning how to stick up for himself, or a closer relationship with a parent. Since, at their core, most stories are about how a character meets a need, getting to know the character's needs readies us to begin thinking about what will happen in the story, and then to write it.

Share Your Writing

Take a look at this entry from my writer's notebook in which I created a character.

My story premise was a girl who is upset because her best friend starts playing with another girl. I should tell you that I came up with this story premise by thinking of one of my writing territories, my daughter, Anzia. When my daughter was younger, she had a similar problem, and it was a really big deal for her. So I figured it would be an interesting problem to give the character, Sarah. I have some experience with the problem and have thought about it a lot.

I began the process of creating a character by asking myself, "What kind of person would have this problem?" First, I came up with the character's name: Sarah. Then I tried to imagine Sarah as a real person. I thought about aspects of her life: her age (she's seven), where she lives, her family members, and what she likes to do. Then I wrote about her.

Most important, I thought about Sarah's problem. I gave her best friend a name: Anna. I decided that they had been best friends since kindergarten, and had been in the same class together since then. And I gave the new girl a name, Jodi, and decided that Anna and Jodi are playing together at recess each day, without Sarah.

Once I figured out all of these things about Sarah, I was ready to think of a story I wanted to tell about her, one in which she has to figure out how she's going to deal with the change in her relationship with her best friend, Anna.

Coach the Student

Even though you have started your story, let's back up a bit and think about your main character.

▶ What is your story premise—your character's problem or conflict?
▶ Tell me some things that would describe a person who has this problem or conflict. What's the character's name? Where does the character live? Who does the character live with? What are the character's likes? Dislikes?
▶ Tell me more about your character's problem or conflict.

◆ Encourage students to draw on what they know when they create characters. Suggest to students that their characters be similar in age and background to themselves and to the kids they know in school. These parameters position students to create characters who they are most likely to write well about.

Link to Student Writing

Writers do certain kinds of work when they get ready to write in a genre. To write short fiction, many writers create characters to tell a story about. Now it's time for you to write about your character in your writer's notebook. Try to think about the aspects of the character as we have discussed.

FOLLOW-UP

▶ Conferences in Book 2: *Drafts* are designed to teach students strategies to further develop their characters while they draft their short story.

▶ Some students want to write science fiction or fantasy stories—sometimes they set them in the "universes" created by other writers (e.g., *Star Wars* stories). Students tend to write science fiction and fantasy stories that are plot heavy, with little character development. This conference can help them, too. It's especially important in these genres to have students write about their main character before they write their stories, and think hard about the problem that the character will deal with. And, when possible, have students connect their life experiences to their main character—even if the character is a Wookie or a Hobbit. (Keep in mind that *Star Wars* is the story of how Luke Skywalker reconciled with his father, Darth Vader.)

SOURCES

I got the idea for this conference from Randy Bomer, who writes about teaching fiction to students in *Time for Meaning: Crafting Literate Lives in Middle & High School* (1995). Lucy Calkins and M. Colleen Cruz also write about this strategy in *Writing Fiction: Big Dreams, Tall Ambitions* (2006).

Sarah:

* Sarah's best friend has started to play with another girl
* Sarah is seven years old
* she lives in Park Slope, Brooklyn
* lives with mom (Julie) and dad (Keith)
* has a younger sister, Lila, who is five
* likes to play soccer, do outdoor sports
* goes to PS 321
* she's in the second grade
* her best friend's name is Anna
* they've been in the same class since kindergarten
* they usually spend recess together every day, and like to kick a soccer ball around the schoolyard.
* the girl Anna has started to play with is Jodi
* Anna and Jodi are now playing together at recess - without Sarah
* Sarah is feeling left out, and doesn't know how to handle the situation

© 2009 by Carl Anderson from *Strategic Writing Conferences* (Portsmouth, NH: Heinemann). This page may be reproduced for classroom use only.

WHAT YOU FIND

The student who could be helped by this conference:

- repeatedly writes about topics in one way.
- always chooses personal narrative when given a choice about what genre to write in.
- feels bored with writing in her writer's notebook because she is tired of writing stories "over and over again."

Exploring a Topic by Writing in a Variety of Ways

CONFERENCE PURPOSE

Teach the student the many ways to write about a topic in her writer's notebook.

MODEL TEXTS

My writer's notebook entries or another writer's notebook entries in which the writer writes about topics in a variety of ways

◆ This is an important conference to have when students are in a unit of study in which they choose the genre. Teaching students to write in a variety of ways—through memories, observations, wonderings, opinions, responses to reading, responses to world events, interesting facts about topics, explorations of ideas, and much, much more—as they explore topics, especially their writing territories, enables them to write about topics from different angles and discover multiple meanings about them. Writing in a variety of ways helps students gather material that can be used to write in many genres.

I'm thrilled that you write entries about topics that really matter to you in your writer's notebook. What I've learned from reading through your notebook, and from talking with you, is that you usually write *in the same way* about topics. I see that most of your entries are stories, things that you've done in your life.

It's good that you gather stories in your writer's notebook—you've got many "seeds" for personal narratives and memoirs. I want to teach you how to write in other ways about your topic. To help you understand how writing in a variety of ways can help you, I want you to imagine a refrigerator that only has lettuce in it, lots and lots of lettuce. Except for salad, there aren't many kinds of meals that your mom or dad could make with lettuce. Now imagine that the refrigerator has eggs, milk, hamburger, pasta, fish, peas, cheese, and many other kinds of food. With a refrigerator filled up with all these kinds of food, your mom or dad could make all sorts of meals.

When you write about a topic in only one way in your writer's notebook, you're probably only going to have the material you need to write in just a few genres. But if you learn how to write in a lot of ways, about a topic that matters to you, then you'll have what you need in order to write in many genres. This is especially important at this point in the school year because you're able to choose the genre you will write in. When you write in a lot of ways, you will have new energy for writing. You won't be limited to one way of thinking—a way that you may not feel like thinking in every day!

Share Your Writing

Take a look through my writer's notebook. I want you to see the variety of ways that I write about topics that matter to me.

This is a memory about my daughter, Anzia, when she was a baby. This entry could be the "seed" for a personal narrative or memoir.

> I was thinking about the time Anzia lost a little alien toy when she was in her stroller. She let out a big scream when she realized it was gone! Since she was inconsolable, we began to retrace the path we had taken through the neighborhood — until, finally, we found it!

Now let me show you a different kind of entry, an opinion that I have about bullying. This entry could be the "seed" for an op-ed.

> I don't think that teachers should look the other way when they realize that a kid is being bullied. That's what happened to me — even when some of my classmates told my teacher what was going on, she said that she couldn't imagine that this could be going on between students in her class.

And here's another kind of entry, a collection of interesting facts about horseshoe crabs.

> I learned today that horseshoe crabs have TEN eyes! And that they serve a really important purpose in the ecosystems of beaches and marshes — they're scavengers, and eat up dead things in the water and on the sand.

Maybe this entry could be the "seed" for a feature article. See, I write in many different ways in my notebook. With all these kinds of entries, I have the material I need to write in many genres.

Explain a Strategy

One way to decide how to write about a topic is to make a web of ways to write it. Take a look at the web I made about one of my writing territories: bullying.

When I started making this web about bullying, I thought about some of the ways writers write about topics in their notebooks. I know that they write memories, so I asked myself, "What is *one time* I remember about bullying?" That question helped me remember two memories—times when I was bullied as a child—and I wrote them in my web.

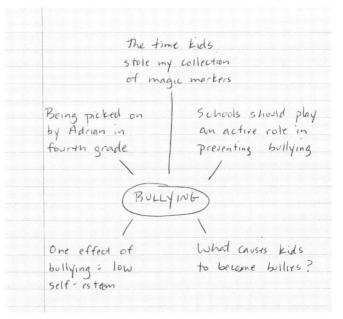

Then, because I know that writers write opinions in their notebooks, I asked myself, "What is *one opinion* that I have about bullying?" That question helped me think of an opinion I have—that schools should play a big role in preventing bullying—and I wrote it on my web.

I know that writers write about the things they know about a topic, so I asked myself, "What is *one thing* I know about bullying?" That question helped me think of something I know—that bullies often suffer from low self-esteem—and I wrote it on my web.

Asking these questions, and others, such as "What questions do I have about bullying?" and "What do I think about bullying?", helped me think in a lot of ways about this one topic. I picked one of the ideas from the web to write about—and I had a lot of other ideas on it for ways to write about bullying later.

Coach the Student

I'd like to help you create a web of ways to write about a topic you care about.

▶ Let's think together about some of the ways you could write about a topic. What's a topic that you know you want to write about?

▶ What is *one time* that you remember about this topic? What is *one opinion* you have about it? What *interesting facts* do you know about it? What *questions* do you have about it?

Link to the Student's Writing

Great, you're imagining different ways to write about your topic. I'd like you to make a web in your notebook now and see if you can come up with even more ways to write about the topic. To help you, I'm going to give you a copy of a list (page 80). Once you've made your web, try writing about your topic in one of the ways suggested on the list. Use ideas from your web.

I want you to remember that you can explore a topic in a lot of different ways in your writer's notebook. Not only will this make writing in your notebook more interesting for you, it will give you options when it comes time to decide which genre to write in.

FOLLOW-UP

Even when students learn to write in a variety of ways about a topic, they still may need help using the material written in the web and in subsequent notebook entries to write in a genre. If this is the case, you'll want to have Book 1: *Topics,* Conference 15, "Selecting a Genre by Considering Interest, Content, or Purpose."

SOURCES

I learned to do this conference from Randy Bomer, who writes about writer's notebooks in *Time for Meaning: Crafting Literate Lives in Middle & High School* (2005). Other educators who have written about the importance of teaching students to write in a variety of ways include Aimee Buckner (*Notebook Know-How: Strategies for the Writer's Notebook*, 2005) and Ralph Fletcher and JoAnn Portalupi (*Lessons for the Writer's Notebook*, 2005).

I was thinking about the time Anzia lost a little alien toy when she was in her stroller. She let out a big scream when she realized it was gone! Since she was inconsolable, we began to retrace the path we had taken through the neighborhood — until, finally, we found it!

© 2009 by Carl Anderson from *Strategic Writing Conferences* (Portsmouth, NH: Heinemann). This page may be reproduced for classroom use only.

I don't think that teachers should look the other way when they realize that a kid is being bullied. That's what happened to me — even when some of my classmates told my teacher what was going on, she said that she couldn't imagine that this could be going on between students in her class.

© 2009 by Carl Anderson from *Strategic Writing Conferences* (Portsmouth, NH: Heinemann). This page may be reproduced for classroom use only.

I learned today that horseshoe crabs have TEN eyes! And that they serve a really important purpose in the ecosystems of beaches and marshes — they're scavengers, and eat up dead things in the water and on the sand.

© 2009 by Carl Anderson from *Strategic Writing Conferences* (Portsmouth, NH: Heinemann). This page may be reproduced for classroom use only.

The time kids
stole my collection
of magic markers

Being picked on
by Adrian in
fourth grade

Schools should play
an active role in
preventing bullying

(BULLYING)

One effect of
bullying: low
self-esteem

What causes kids
to become bullies?

© 2009 by Carl Anderson from *Strategic Writing Conferences* (Portsmouth, NH: Heinemann). This page may be reproduced for classroom use only.

Ways to Write about a Topic in My Writer's Notebook

▸ Write stories that are connected to the topic.

▸ Write about facts that interest me about the topic.

▸ Write about what I wonder about the topic.

▸ Write opinions I have about the topic.

▸ Write about the ideas I have about the topic.

▸ Write a careful description of some aspect of the topic.

▸ Write about ideas for fictional stories about the topic.

▸ Write about why the topic is important to me.

© 2009 by Carl Anderson from *Strategic Writing Conferences* (Portsmouth, NH: Heinemann). This page may be reproduced for classroom use only.

PART THREE

✳ developing topics

14

Selecting a Topic by Considering Interest, Audience, or Occasion

WHAT YOU FIND
The student who could be helped by this conference:
- has decided to write a draft about a topic that isn't in his writer's notebook.
- has made a quick choice of a topic—without reading through his notebook and considering several possible topics.
- has not been able to select an entry and doesn't seem to understand why he would pick one entry over another, or even why he needs to select an entry in the first place.

CONFERENCE PURPOSE
Teach the student to choose a seed topic by considering interest, audience, and occasion—before he writes a draft that he will share with others.

You are at an exciting step in the writing process. Let's take a look at the topics you have brainstormed and explored in your writer's notebook. I want to talk with you about how to choose a seed topic that you will be excited to write about, and eventually publish a piece about. Even if you already think you know what you want to write about, it's worth thinking about that choice again.

When writers select a seed topic, they make careful choices. They take the time to read through many, if not all, the entries in their writer's notebook. And when they read each entry, they ask themselves, "Do I want to pick *this* topic as my seed topic—the one I'll grow into a full draft?"

Explain a Strategy

One way that we choose a topic is by considering how interested in it we are. We might decide to pick a topic as a seed because we are passionate about it and want to put time, energy, and creativity into developing that seed into a draft.

We might pick a topic as a seed because we can imagine an audience who will love to read about it—friends, family, classmates, or members of our community—and we want to write a draft to share with them.

And another way that we choose a topic to grow into a draft is by thinking about whether there are any occasions in the near future when we could share a piece of writing about the topic. For example, sometimes writers will pick a particular topic because it relates to a special person in their life whose birthday is coming up and they want to write something for that person, or they choose a seed because a holiday is approaching and they want to write a piece to share on that day.

Picking a seed idea is a big decision. It's worth taking the time to carefully consider which topic to write about.

Coach the Student

Let's look through some of your notebook entries and think about which topics are good candidates to be a seed topic. As you consider a topic, ask yourself these questions:

▶ Does this topic really interest me? Am I passionate about it?

▶ Are there people with whom I would like to share my ideas about this topic?

▶ Is there an occasion approaching that makes me want to create a piece about this topic?

Let's read another entry and think about whether it would make a good seed topic. Ask yourself the three questions to help you make your decision.

◆ If a person or group in a student's life might be a good audience for a topic, or if an important occasion is approaching that would suit a topic, be sure to mention it.

Link to the Student's Writing

I'm going to leave you to read the rest of your writer's notebook by yourself. Read each entry carefully. Keep asking yourself, "Do I want to pick *this* topic as my seed topic?"

Remember that whenever you're trying to select a seed topic for a piece of writing, it's worth taking the time to make a thoughtful decision. Consider your interest in the topic, audience, and occasion to help you decide.

SOURCES
Katie Wood Ray's discussion (*Wondrous Words: Writers and Writing in the Elementary Classroom*, 1999, pages 95–101) of the reasons why writers choose a topic for a writing project inspired this conference.

15

Selecting a Genre by Considering Interest, Content, or Purpose

WHAT YOU FIND

The student who could be helped by this conference has the option to choose both the topic and genre for his next piece of writing but:

- is not sure which genre she wants to write in.
- is used to being told which genre to write in.
- seems paralyzed by the opportunity to choose a genre.

CONFERENCE PURPOSE

Teach the student to choose a genre that matches her interest, content, or purpose.

◆ A well-designed writing-workshop curriculum includes units of study in which students choose the kind of writing they will do. In a craft, punctuation, or grammar study, it isn't necessary for all students to write in the same genre. They give us the opportunity to teach students how to choose a genre to write in—something they will do many times in their lives. For information about how to design these studies, see Katie Wood Ray's *Study Driven: A Framework for Planning Units of Study in the Writing Workshop* (2006), Janet Angelillo's *A Fresh Approach to Teaching Punctuation* (2002) and *Grammar Study* (2008), and Dan Feigelson's *Practical Punctuation: Lessons on Rule Making and Rule Breaking in Elementary Writing* (2008).

IT SURE IS AN EXCITING TIME of the year, isn't it, because *you* get to choose the kind of writing you're going to do. I can tell that you're not quite sure which genre you want to write in, though. I want to teach you how writers choose a genre.

Explain a Strategy

Sometimes we decide to write in a particular genre because the writing we have done in our writer's notebook already resembles that genre. For example, if you have several entries about things that you and your best friend have done together, and you feel like developing them, then it may make sense to write a personal narrative or memoir, or even a narrative poem. Or, if you have gathered information in your notebook about skiing tricks and you think it would be fun to develop them, it may make sense to write a feature article. In these cases, you decide the genre to write in *after* you pick the seed topic from your writer's notebook.

Sometimes we simply love a certain genre and want to write in it again and again. For example, some writers spend much of their lives writing poetry or fiction. They return to the genre because it fits what they want to say. If you are like them, you would think about the genres you have enjoyed reading and writing in. Then you would look for an entry in your writer's notebook that could be a seed for a piece in the genre you have chosen. You might also gather new material in your notebook that you could use to write in the genre. For example, if you love writing memoirs, you would reread your entries, looking for stories from your life that could be seeds for memoirs, and you would write more stories in your notebook in order to gather material for writing memoirs.

Other times, writers have a purpose that compels them to write, and a certain genre makes sense because it helps convey their message. For example, someone who wants a law to be passed to put a traffic light at a dangerous intersection might write a letter to a government official or write an op-ed in the newspaper. If you were writing for a purpose like this, you would reread your notebook entries for material that you could use in the piece. If you found you didn't have the material you need, you would gather it in your notebook. Then you would use it to fulfill your purpose for writing.

Even when writers have decided which genre to write in, they may not be ready to write a draft right away. They may still need to use strategies to develop the seed topic. Which strategies they use depends on the genre they've chosen.

Coach the Student

I'd like to help you choose which genre to write in by asking you some questions.

▶ Have you already selected a seed entry that you want to turn into a piece of writing? Does the kind of entry you've chosen suggest a certain genre?

▶ Do you have a favorite genre in which you want to write? Do you think you have the material you need in your notebook to write in this genre, or do you need to gather the material you need before you start drafting?

▶ Is there a reason why you want to write a piece? What genre do other writers usually write in when they have this purpose? Do you think you have the material you need in your notebook to write in this genre—and to satisfy your purpose—or do you need to gather the material you need before you start drafting?

Link to the Student's Writing

I'd like you to take some time to think about the different ways of choosing a genre (considering interest in a genre, content, and purpose) for your next piece of writing. After you decide which genre you're going to write in, you'll be ready to develop your seed topic.

Remember that writers choose to write in a genre for several reasons. If you keep those reasons in mind, I have no doubt that you'll make the right choice of genre.

SOURCES

Katie Wood Ray's thinking (*Wondrous Words: Writers and Writing in the Elementary Classroom,* 1999, pages 95–101) about how writers move toward writing projects helped me design this conference.

16

Developing a Topic by Reflecting on Its Significance

WHAT YOU FIND

The student who could be helped by this conference is writing about a topic that matters to her, but she:

- has not reflected on the topic's significance.
- is having trouble articulating the meaning behind the topic.
- doesn't yet have a clear sense of the meaning she wants to convey—and so is unsure of which parts of her topic to focus on and develop.

CONFERENCE PURPOSE

Teach the student to reflect on the significance of a topic in order to develop it in writing.

MODEL TEXT

My writer's notebook entry or another writer's notebook entry that includes reflective writing about a topic

◆ View this conference on *Carl on Camera: Modeling Strategic Writing Conferences* DVD.

I SEE THAT YOU'RE EXCITED about the seed topic you've picked, and you're developing it in your notebook to get ready to write a draft about it. Good work! I want to show you a new—and very important—way to use your writer's notebook, which is to think about why a seed topic is important to you.

Experienced writers use their notebooks to *reflect* on the topics they write entries about, especially the ones they select as seeds. They reflect by asking themselves, "Why is this topic important to me?" And then they write to answer this question.

Reflecting on the topic helps us think about what we want to say to readers in our draft. When we have some sense of what we want to say before we begin a draft, we can better decide how to craft it—which parts to focus on, which parts to leave out, and which parts to develop the most.

It was the last first day of school at PS 321 for Anzia and us this year. Weird. All the same routines — taking a picture of her outside school ("Do I HAVE to?" Anzia complained, a little louder than in previous years.). Going together into the school's backyard, mobbed with kids and parents. (Anzia moved ahead of us a little bit faster than in previous years.). Finding Anzia's class (Anzia ignored me once she was with her friends.). And watching her go upstairs with her class, suddenly out of sight, gone — a fifth grader.

Share Your Writing

I want to show you how I reflected on a seed topic in my writer's notebook. Soon after Anzia's first day of fifth grade, I wrote an entry about how she seemed more interested in seeing her friends that morning than being with her little brother and me.

When I selected this entry as a seed for a draft, I reflected on the importance of the morning. I had to think deeper about this experience, not just relive it in my mind to remember all of the details, but also think about how I was feeling and what the experience meant to me. I reflected on these things by

> Why is this topic important to me? Although it was the first day of school, I felt it was the first day of a long series of goodbyes that we'll make this year. Goodbye to first days of school at PS 321 (for Anzia, at least!) Goodbye to the familiar routines, the familiar building. Goodbye to fifth grade, to elementary school.
>
> And goodbye to Anzia's childhood ... Yesterday she was a nervous kindergartener – today she's a confident fifth grader. Tomorrow? Yesterday she clung to me tightly – today she prefers her friends.

writing a new entry, one that I began with the question, "Why is this topic important to me?"

Writing about how I was feeling on Anzia's first day of fifth grade helped me think about the deeper meaning. It helped me know what I wanted to *say* about the experience. I realized that I wanted my story to show how part of being a parent is saying a series of good-byes to your child as the child grows older. Realizing what I wanted to say about the topic, its significance, helped me make a lot of smart decisions about how to write the draft about the experience.

Coach the Student

I'd like to help you try to determine the significance of a topic. Let's look at an entry in your writer's notebook that is the seed for a story you want to write and publish.

▶ I'd like you to think *out loud* about your answer to the question "Why is this topic important to me?" It might take you awhile to figure out the answer.

Link to the Student's Writing

Now it's time for you to try this strategy in your writer's notebook. Take some time to write a response to the question, "Why is this topic important to me?"

Remember that this strategy is something that experienced writers are in the habit of doing frequently in their notebooks, especially when they need to develop a seed topic. That's my hope for you— that reflecting on the topic you want to write about before you start drafting becomes a habit.

FOLLOW-UP

It's worth repeating this conference whenever students are picking seed topics until reflecting on the significance of a topic becomes habitual. This conference is very important. Students who begin the drafting process with a sense of what they want to say are positioned to make smart decisions about how to proceed. You can teach students to use this strategy in any genre.

SOURCES

The thinking of Donald Murray (*Write to Learn*, 2004) and Randy Bomer (*Time for Meaning: Crafting Literate Lives in Middle & High School*, 1995)—about writing to discover meaning about a topic—helped me to develop this conference.

It was the last first day of school at PS 321 for Anzia and us this year. Weird. All the same routines — taking a picture of her outside school ("DO I HAVE to?" Anzia complained, a little louder than in previous years.). Going together into the school's backyard, mobbed with kids and parents. (Anzia moved ahead of us a little bit faster than in previous years.). Finding Anzia's class (Anzia ignored me once she was with her friends.). And watching her go upstairs with her class, suddenly out of sight, gone — a fifth grader.

© 2009 by Carl Anderson from *Strategic Writing Conferences* (Portsmouth, NH: Heinemann). This page may be reproduced for classroom use only.

Why is this topic important to me?. Although
it was the first day of school, I felt it
was the first day of a long series of goodbyes
that we'll make this year. Goodbye to first
days of school at PS 321 (for Anzia, at least!)
Goodbye to the familiar routines, the familiar
building. Goodbye to fifth grade, to elementary
school.

And goodbye to Anzia's childhood ... Yesterday
she was a nervous kindergartener — today she's
a confident fifth grader. Tomorrow? Yesterday
she clung to me tightly — today she prefers
her friends.

© 2009 by Carl Anderson from *Strategic Writing Conferences* (Portsmouth, NH: Heinemann). This page may be reproduced for classroom use only.

17

Developing a Topic by Finding a Focusing Line

WHAT YOU FIND

The student who could be helped by this conference:

- has not yet thought about what he wants to say.
- intends to write an entry in which he reflects on the meaning of the topic.
- has written a line (or several lines) in his seed entry in which he has reflected about the significance of a topic, but he is unaware that he has done the reflection.

CONFERENCE PURPOSE

Teach the student to find a focusing line about a topic that can help him write a more focused draft.

MODEL TEXTS

My writer's notebook entries or another writer's notebook entries with a clear focusing line

I SEE THAT YOU HAVE written entries about your topic, but you aren't sure exactly what you want to say about it. I want to teach you a strategy that writers use to help them figure out the meaning of a topic, a strategy that a great writer named Don Murray calls "finding a focusing line." When writers reread their entries, they can sometimes identify a line that really says what the meaning is behind their topic. This is the "focusing line," and it helps us answer the question "What do I want to say about this topic?" When we know what we want to say, we are better able to write a story that conveys this meaning to readers clearly and thoughtfully.

Share Your Writing

Take a look at an entry that I wrote in my writer's notebook about going boating with my dad. In this entry I discovered a great focusing line—the line that helped me realize the meaning that I wanted to share with my readers.

When I wrote this entry, I wanted to capture the memory of the first time that my dad let me steer his motorboat. Later, when I reread the entry, I found myself lingering over one line I had written.

> *In that moment, I was filled with a sense of adventure that I rarely felt during the everyday life I led in the suburbs.*

As I reread the line, I realized that it was a focusing line. It's not a detail about the memory; it's my reflection about *why* going out with my dad in his boat was important to me. When I find a focusing line like this one, I think of it as a great discovery. This one line

> My dad sure loved taking us out in his motorboat. It was tiny, just sixteen feet long with a 40 horsepower engine on the stern, but to us kids, it seemed like the Queen Elizabeth. I remember the day when dad let me steer the boat all by myself out of the canal onto the bay. It took my breath away when we reached the end of the canal. The Great South Bay stretched out ahead of us, sunlight sparkling everywhere on the waves. In that moment, I was filled with a sense of adventure that I rarely felt during the everyday life I led in the suburbs. My dad said, "Open up the throttle!", the bow of boat lifted out of the water, and off we went towards that day's adventure.

> In that moment, I was filled with a sense of adventure that I rarely felt during the everyday life I led in the suburbs. Adventure... my sisters and I never quite knew what to expect from my dad. A visit to an island in the middle of the bay? A trip to the Captree Bridge, ten miles down the bay? On the Great South Bay, my sense of the world was bigger than it was home on our sleepy suburban street. On my dad's boat, I had the feeling that someday, as "captain" of my own life, I could go to places wonderful and unexpected, too.

◆ When the student has difficulty locating a focusing line as she rereads her entries, point out a line that you think is a good candidate and ask if she agrees. Explain why you feel it is a focusing line.

sums up what I wanted to share with readers about the importance of this experience: The times when I went boating with my dad were moments of real adventure in my childhood, in contrast to my routine, somewhat boring, day-to-day suburban life.

Once I found this focusing line, I used it to help me think further about the meaning. I wrote the line on top of a new page in my writer's notebook, and used it as a starting place to think even more about it.

Explain a Strategy

Here's how to read the entries you've written about your topic and look for focusing lines. As you read, ask yourself, "Can I find a line that helps answer the question, 'Why is this topic important for me?'" Most of the lines written in entries are about the details of a story. But, occasionally, we come across a line that answers this question. That's the focusing line.

Coach the Student

I'd like to help you search for a focusing line in your entry. I'm going to sit with you as you reread the entry.

▶ When you encounter a line that answers the question, "Why is this topic important to me?", stop and read the line to me.

▶ Let's discuss why you think it's a good focusing line.

Link to the Student's Writing

I'd like you to read over the rest of the entry, as well as the other ones you've written about the topic, and see if you find any other focusing lines. Underline them when you find them. Then pick the one that best helps you think about what you want to say about your topic. Write it at the top of a new page in your notebook, and then use it as a starting point to reflect even more about the significance of your topic.

Keep this strategy in mind when you want to focus your draft on the deeper meaning of the topic. Sometimes we've already thought about the significance of a topic without even realizing it!

FOLLOW-UP

Teach students to look for a focusing line whenever they are getting ready to write a draft—in any genre.

SOURCES

Experienced writers often reflect on the significance of the topics they write about in their notebooks *as* they write about them. As they reread their entries about a topic, they search for a line that helps them think about what they want to say in a draft. Don Murray (***Write to Learn,*** 2004) calls this kind of line the ***focusing line.*** Writes Murray, "The [focusing] line gives the writer the energy to pursue the potential meaning that lies within the as-yet-unwritten draft . . . [It] ignites the draft."

My dad sure loved taking us out in his motorboat. It was tiny, just sixteen feet long with a 40 horsepower engine on the stern, but to us kids, it seemed like the Queen Elizabeth. I remember the day when dad let me steer the boat all by myself out of the canal onto the bay. It took my breath away when we reached the end of the canal. The Great South Bay stretched out ahead of us, sunlight sparkling everywhere on the waves. In that moment, I was filled with a sense of adventure that I rarely felt during the everyday life I led in the suburbs. My dad said, "Open up the throttle!," the bow of boat lifted out of the water, and off we went towards that day's adventure.

© 2009 by Carl Anderson from *Strategic Writing Conferences* (Portsmouth, NH: Heinemann). This page may be reproduced for classroom use only.

In that moment, I was filled with a sense of adventure that I rarely felt during the everyday life I led in the suburbs. Adventure... my sisters and I never quite knew what to expect from my dad. A visit to an island in the middle of the bay? A trip to the Captree Bridge, ten miles down the bay? On the Great South Bay, my sense of the world was bigger than it was home on our sleepy suburban street. On my dad's boat, I had the feeling that someday, as "captain" of my own life, I could go to places wonderful and unexpected, too.

© 2009 by Carl Anderson from *Strategic Writing Conferences* (Portsmouth, NH: Heinemann). This page may be reproduced for classroom use only.

18

Developing a Topic by Sketching

The student who could be helped by this conference typically writes vague stories without concrete details.

CONFERENCE PURPOSE

Teach the student to develop a seed topic by sketching aspects of it in his writer's notebook.

MODEL TEXTS

Marshfield Dreams by Ralph Fletcher

My sketches from my writer's notebook or another writer's sketches

I CAN TELL THAT you're excited to write your story. You have selected your seed topic, and you feel ready to begin writing your draft. I want to teach you a strategy for developing a topic that will help you write a draft that contains many precise details. The strategy is to sketch parts of the story.

Have you ever wondered how fiction writers like J.K. Rowling are able to write so that we can "see" the places they write about—like Hogwarts—even though they don't exist? Or how writers like Ralph Fletcher are able to write so vividly that we can "see" the places where they grew up—even though we've never been to the places? It's the details in a piece of writing that help us create a picture in our minds of the places and characters.

Before we can write with detail, we have to be able to "see" the elements of the story in our own mind. One way we can recall stories that have happened to us or imagine fictional stories is to sketch. Sketching parts of a story helps us remember or imagine lots of details that we can write into a draft.

What do we sketch? We can sketch the main character—and other characters, too—to help us remember or imagine what they look like. Sometimes we sketch the main character doing something in the story, such as sledding down a hill. Sometimes we sketch the main character in the middle of the story's conflict, for example, having a fight with a sibling.

Other times, we sketch the setting of a story—or several settings, if the story happens in a couple of places. Some writers even make maps, real or fictional, of the place they're writing about. Author Ralph Fletcher included a map in the first pages of his memoir,

Marshfield Dreams. Drawing this map helped Fletcher remember details of the setting, details that he included in many of his stories.

We can also sketch objects that are important in a story—a boat that the characters travel on or a rocket ship the characters zoom around space in. By taking the time to sketch before writing, we are better able to "see" our story before we write, and that gives us ideas for details to include in our draft.

◆ Sketching is a marvelous strategy to teach students who like to write fantasy or science fiction. Sketching the aliens or wizards that populate these stories, or the objects of power or the spaceships, can help students write about them in a more believable way.

Share Your Writing

I want to show you some sketching I did before writing a story about a time I chased—and finally captured—a giant toad at Tobay Beach on Long Island when I was a boy.

I made a couple of sketches. The first one is a map of the beach, which helped me remember where all the different things happened. The second one is the scene where I am chasing the toad. This was an important scene in the story, and drawing it helped me remember details about the chase.

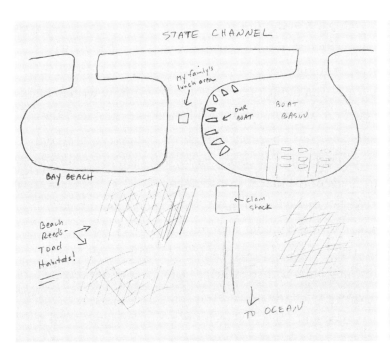

Explain a Strategy

To help you sketch before writing your story, I'm going to give you a list of story elements that writers sketch (page 102). However, it isn't necessary to sketch every one of these story elements before you draft. Ask yourself the question, "What elements of the story are *important* for me to sketch?" The answer to this question is often a significant character or scene, or a setting or object that you want readers to "see" clearly in their minds when they read your story.

Coach the Student

Let's imagine what you might sketch that will help you "see" a part of your story better before you write it.

▶ What part of your story could you sketch that would help you remember or imagine the details?

▶ What important characters might you sketch to help you describe what they look like?

▶ Is there a setting you might sketch to help you describe the details of it?

▶ Is there an important object in your story that sketching could help you think about?

Link to the Student's Writing

I'd like for you to sketch now. Keep in mind that writers usually use some strategies that help them "see" the story in their minds and help them write details. Sketching is a strategy you can use whenever you're getting ready to write a draft.

◆ If the student is new to sketching, you might try to nudge him to sketching one, maybe two elements of his story. Or, based on your ongoing assessment of his narrative writing, nudge him to sketch a particular element of a story, like the setting, that you would like him to develop further.

FOLLOW-UP

▶ In a subsequent conference, you may need to help students make use of sketches as they draft. Suggest that they write a list of important details about a character or a setting next to a sketch and then try to use them in their draft.

▶ Teach students to sketch as a revision strategy. When students are revising a section of a draft, suggest that they sketch what is happening in that part. See if they can come up with some new details to add to that part of their draft.

▶ You can also teach students who are writing in other genres to use this strategy. For example, a student who is writing a feature article about types of sailboats might write about them with more precise detail if he sketches them first.

STATE CHANNEL

BOAT BASIN

OUR BOAT

My family's lunch area

clam shack

TO OCEAN

BAY BEACH

Beach Reeds — Toad Habitats!

© 2009 by Carl Anderson from *Strategic Writing Conferences* (Portsmouth, NH: Heinemann). This page may be reproduced for classroom use only.

© 2009 by Carl Anderson from *Strategic Writing Conferences* (Portsmouth, NH: Heinemann). This page may be reproduced for classroom use only.

Story Elements I Can Sketch

◗ main character

◗ secondary characters

◗ main character experiencing the story's conflict

◗ object important to the story

◗ map or view of the setting

◗ important scene

© 2009 by Carl Anderson from *Strategic Writing Conferences* (Portsmouth, NH: Heinemann). This page may be reproduced for classroom use only.

19

Developing a Topic by Thinking Deeply about the Story's Conflict

WHAT YOU FIND

The student who could be helped by this conference has written an entry in his writer's notebook that:

- is a focused moment but lacks an obvious central conflict or problem.
- describes the main character's characteristics but not the character's conflict.

CONFERENCE PURPOSE

Teach the student to develop the conflict of a story.

MODEL TEXT

My writer's notebook entry or another writer's notebook entry that includes writing about the conflict of a story

I CAN SEE THAT you've chosen a seed for a story. It's tricky to figure out how to make it an exciting story, right? You're going to need to do some thinking about the story's *conflict* before you draft. At the center of a good story—a story that grabs a reader's attention—is a *conflict*. That means that the main character is having some kind of problem or trouble.

Sometimes the main character has a conflict with another character. That's the kind of conflict that author Patricia Polacco describes in *My Rotten Redheaded Older Brother*. She tells how her brother always outdid her in everything, and how she was determined to feel special by outdoing him in something.

Sometimes the main character has a conflict with some *thing* in the world, like a steep mountain that she is climbing or a baseball he is trying to hit. That's the kind of conflict that author Donald Crews describes in *Shortcut*. The kids in the story encounter a train that almost kills them.

Sometimes the main character has an internal conflict, which means she is trying to face a part of herself that is causing problems. That's the kind of conflict that Maurice Sendak describes in *Where The Wild Things Are*. Max struggles to tame the wild impulses that get him in trouble with his mom.

How do writers figure out what the conflict will be in their story? They think about the kind of conflict the main character has, why the character has the conflict, why it's a challenge to deal with the conflict, and what the main character does, or could do, to overcome it. Writers do this kind of thinking when they write a true story—a personal narrative—as well as when they write a fictional story.

Share Your Writing

Take a look at an entry in my writer's notebook in which I thought about the conflict. I wanted to write about a time when I caught a big toad at the beach when I was a boy. Before I wrote the draft, I wrote this entry to help me identify and understand the story's conflict.

"The Great Toad Hunt"

- The conflict in this story is me versus a huge toad, human versus amphibian. A bit like Moby Dick, Ahab versus the whale.
- When I first saw the toad, it was important for me to catch him because I wanted to impress my parents and sisters. Later on in the story, I wanted to catch the toad so that I could prove to my family that he really existed - and wasn't fibbing about seeing a giant toad!
- It was hard to end this conflict because the toad was quick, incredibly quick. Almost like a cat - that fast. He was so speedy that the first time I chased him, he got away. I guess to have gotten that big, he must have been very good at evading predators.
- I was finally able to resolve the me versus toad conflict by outsmarting him - I chased him towards a wall of thick reeds that he couldn't get past, and he was trapped. Finally, the toad was mine!

As I wrote, I figured out the type of conflict I experienced in the story. It was "me versus the toad," slow-footed human versus super-quick amphibian! I wrote about why resolving this conflict was important to me—I really wanted to catch the toad so I could impress my family. I wrote about why I was having trouble solving the problem—the toad was incredibly quick, and I just wasn't fast enough to catch up to it. And I wrote about how I ultimately solved the problem—I realized that I would need to corner the toad in a place where he couldn't jump away from me.

By doing this thinking about the conflict, I came up with the basic outline of the story. The plot of a story, after all, is the series of actions that a main character takes to resolve a conflict. Doing this thinking helped me think about what the story was really about, the deeper meaning: a boy who wanted to impress his family.

Explain a Strategy

The questions I asked myself are the same questions that many writers ask themselves when thinking about the conflict of a story they want to write. I'm going to give you a list of these questions (page 107). As you write an entry in your writer's notebook about the conflict in your story, read over the list of questions. The questions will give you ideas for writing about the conflict before you write the story.

Coach the Student

I'd like to help you think about the main character's conflict.

▶ What is the problem that your character is having?

▶ Why does your character have this problem?

- Why is it important for your main character to solve the problem?
- What makes it hard for your character to solve the problem?
- How did the main character resolve the problem?

Link to the Student's Writing

Try writing about your story's conflict in your writer's notebook. Remember that conflict is at the heart of a good story, and that writers take time to develop their main character's conflict before they write a draft.

FOLLOW-UP

- Conference 15 in Book 2: *Drafts*, "Crafting a Lead by Creating Tension," teaches students to establish tension at the beginning of a story by showing the main character's conflict or problem.

SOURCES

For further reading on conflict in a story, read Ralph Fletcher's writing on narrative tension in *What a Writer Needs* (1993, Ch. 9).

"The Great Toad Hunt"

- The conflict in this story is me versus a huge toad, human versus amphibian. A bit like Moby Dick, Ahab versus the whale.
- When I first saw the toad, it was important for me to catch him because I wanted to impress my parents and sisters. Later on in the story, I wanted to catch the toad so that I could prove to my family that he really existed - and wasn't fibbing about seeing a giant toad!
- It was hard to end this conflict because the toad was quick, incredibly quick. Almost like a cat - that fast. He was so speedy that the first time I chased him, he got away. I guess to have gotten that big, he must have been very good at evading predators.
- I was finally able to resolve the me versus toad conflict by outsmarting him - I chased him towards a wall of thick reeds that he couldn't get past, and he was trapped. Finally, the toad was mine!

© 2009 by Carl Anderson from *Strategic Writing Conferences* (Portsmouth, NH: Heinemann). This page may be reproduced for classroom use only.

Questions about My Story's Conflict

▶ What is the main character's conflict?

▶ Why does the character have this conflict?

▶ Why is resolving the conflict important to the character?

▶ What is preventing the character from resolving the conflict?

▶ What needs to happen for the character to resolve the conflict?

© 2009 by Carl Anderson from *Strategic Writing Conferences* (Portsmouth, NH: Heinemann). This page may be reproduced for classroom use only.

20

Developing a Character by Envisioning and Writing

WHAT YOU FIND

The student who could be helped by this conference plans to write a personal narrative, memoir, or short story but:

- needs help developing her main character on paper—even if this character is herself—as well as the secondary characters.

CONFERENCE PURPOSE

Teach the student to develop characters by envisioning and then writing about them.

MODEL TEXT

My writer's notebook entry or another writer's notebook entry that includes detailed writing about a character

◆ Well-developed characters don't spring out of thin air. Long before many stories are drafted, writers **envision** their characters. They think about what they look like, how they talk, what they think about, what their dreams are, and what makes them unique. In fact, many fiction writers come to think of their characters as real people who have "come alive" during the writing of a story. And writers of personal narrative and memoir are satisfied only when the real people who they write about "come alive" on the page for readers.

I'M GLAD TO SEE THAT you're excited about writing your story. I want to talk to you about an important kind of work that writers do before they write. They think about and develop their characters.

Characters are such an important part of a story. We read stories—both true stories and fiction stories—to get to know characters. As we read a well-written story, we come to care deeply about the characters. What happens to the characters affects us. We laugh or cry, we are inspired to think about grand ideas, and we reflect on our lives. It's a real challenge for writers to "bring their characters to life" for readers.

Before they start writing stories, writers often spend time writing about the characters in their writer's notebook. When we are writing a true story—for example, a personal narrative or memoir—we envision and write about the characters to help us remember details about them. We can include these details in our story so that the characters seem real to our readers.

When we write fictional stories, envisioning and writing about the characters help us imagine them clearly enough to write about them with lots of detail. Again, the characters seem real to us when we read about them.

Share Your Writing

I want to show you some work I did in my writer's notebook to get ready to write a story about an ill-fated boat trip that my dad took my sisters and me on one night on Long Island's Great South Bay. In the story, my dad played a major role, so I thought it was

Dad :
- Kenneth Valentine Anderson
- 46 years old, at the time of the story
- fun-loving, sometimes irresponsible (lost
  track of time, such as the time we needed
  to leave the beach before it got too dark
  to cross the bay in the boat)
- very casual in appearance - ratty t-shirt,
  bathing suit
- big pot belly - his bathing suit had trouble
  staying up
- had a bunch of favorite sayings, such as
  "you lazy loafer!"
- loved going out in his boat with his three kids
- loved his little boat, going clamming and to
  the beach
- Dad missed the island he grew up on in Maine-
  Vinalhaven. I think going out in the boat
  reminded him of the place he considered
  his true home
- I think dad's fun-loving side was in conflict
  with being a responsible parent. Losing track
  of time at the beach put his three kids in
  danger when we crossed the bay in the dark!

important that I do some thinking and writing about him before I started drafting.

Before I wrote this entry, I closed my eyes and pictured my dad in my mind. Then, after I had a clear picture of him, I asked myself some basic questions about him. You can see that I wrote down the answers to these questions—his name, how old I think he was when this story took place. Then I dug into my memory a little deeper, and I asked myself about his personality, because it was his personality that got us into trouble that night! I then wrote about his personality, and I also did some writing about what he looked like. This writing is a bit embarrassing, because he had a really, really big pot belly when I was a kid. And I wrote about a number of other things, too—the gestures he used to make, his laugh, the little details that made him unique.

Writing this entry about my dad gave me a clear picture of him in my mind, and that helped me write well about him when I wrote the draft of the story.

Explain a Strategy

When writers develop a character in their writer's notebook, they envision the character and ask themselves questions about the character. If they're writing about a real person, these questions help them remember details. If they're writing about a fictional character, these questions help them imagine details.

I'm going to give you a list of questions that you can ask yourself anytime you're developing a character for a story (page 112). Read through the list, pick the ones that you think will help you write about the character, and then jot down your answers to the questions in your writer's notebook.

Coach the Student

I'd like to help you think about how you can develop a detailed character for your story by envisioning and asking questions.

▶ Close your eyes and picture the character in your mind.

▶ Tell me about the character. What is the character's name? Describe the character.

Link to the Student's Writing

Continue thinking about the main character and start writing about the character in your writer's notebook. This will help you write a really good draft of your story that includes vivid details about the main character.

Remember that writers envision their characters before they write. Doing this helps them write with detail that make the characters "come alive" for readers.

FOLLOW-UP

▶ In a follow-up conference, teach students to use the same envisioning and questioning strategy to develop secondary characters.

▶ When students write a draft, they often don't know how to use the details they come up with about a character. Conference 25 in Book 2: *Drafts*, "Crafting a Scene by Using Defining Details to Create a Vivid Character," helps students use the details they gather.

SOURCES

I learned to do this conference after hearing Randy Bomer speak about writing fiction at the Teachers College Reading and Writing Project (TCRWP) Summer Institute in 1992. He subsequently wrote about it in *Time for Meaning: Crafting Literate Lives in Middle & High School* (1995). Nancie Atwell discusses writing fiction in *In the Middle: New Understandings About Writing, Reading, and Learning* (1998), as do Lucy Calkins and M. Colleen Cruz in *Writing Fiction: Big Dreams, Tall Ambitions* (2006). Ralph Fletcher has an excellent chapter on creating characters in *What A Writer Needs* (1993, ch. 5).

Dad:
- Kenneth Valentine Anderson
- 46 years old, at the time of the story
- fun-loving, sometimes irresponsible (lost track of time, such as the time we needed to leave the beach before it got too dark to cross the bay in the boat)
- very casual in appearance — ratty t-shirt, bathing suit
- big pot belly — his bathing suit had trouble staying up
- had a bunch of favorite sayings, such as "you lazy loafer!"
- loved going out in his boat with his three kids
- loved his little boat, going clamming and to the beach
- Dad missed the island he grew up on in Maine—Vinalhaven. I think going out in the boat reminded him of the place he considered his true home
- I think dad's fun-loving side was in conflict with being a responsible parent. Losing track of time at the beach put his three kids in danger when we crossed the bay in the dark!

© 2009 by Carl Anderson from *Strategic Writing Conferences* (Portsmouth, NH: Heinemann). This page may be reproduced for classroom use only.

Questions to Help Me Develop a Character

▶ What is the character's name?

▶ How old is the character?

▶ What is the character's personality?

▶ What does the character look like?

▶ How does the character talk?

▶ What gestures does the character usually make?

▶ What is the character's family background?

▶ Who are the important people in the character's life?

▶ What does the character like? Dislike?

▶ What does the character care about?

▶ What is the character afraid of?

▶ What are the character's dreams?

▶ What makes the character unique?

▶ What problem (or problems) does the character have?

© 2009 by Carl Anderson from *Strategic Writing Conferences* (Portsmouth, NH: Heinemann). This page may be reproduced for classroom use only.

Developing the Setting by Adding Sensory Details

WHAT YOU FIND
The student who could be helped by this conference:
- has written about the setting in a seed entry in a vague or general way.
- has not written about the setting at all.

CONFERENCE PURPOSE

Teach the student to use the five senses to imagine and describe the setting of a story.

MODEL TEXT

My writer's notebook entry or another writer's notebook entry that contains detailed writing about a setting

IN THE WRITING YOU'VE DONE so far in your writer's notebook, I can see that you've done a lot of thinking about what happens in your story, but you've only written a few details about the setting—where and when the story takes place. I want to teach you a strategy for getting a much more detailed picture in your mind of the setting. Then, you'll be able to write about the setting so vividly that your readers will feel like they are there.

Writers include *setting* details as a "backdrop" to the story, to help readers imagine the place where characters are doing things. Setting details can also create a mood and help readers understand the characters' actions and feelings.

Setting details don't magically flow from our pen when we draft. We have to envision the setting of our story; that is, we have to get a detailed picture of it in our mind before we draft. One strategy that we use to do this is the "five senses" strategy. Thinking about what we see, hear, smell, touch, and even taste in a setting helps us write details in our story.

Share Your Writing

I want to show you how I used the "five senses" strategy in my writer's notebook. I used it to get ready to write a story about watching my son, Haskell, climb the monkey bars in the playground for the first time.

First, I made a list of the five senses: sight, sound, smell, touch, and taste. Then, next to each sense, I brainstormed setting details. I closed my eyes and imagined that I was at the playground again on that day. I tried to remember what I experienced for each sense and came up with a great list of details about my setting, the playground on that afternoon. Using the strategy sure helped me gather specific setting details for my entry, didn't it?

After this brainstorming, I reread the entry and thought about which details to use in my draft. I thought some details would help readers imagine the setting, like the detail about the playground equipment and the hundreds of children running around. I thought these would be good backdrop setting details, so I wrote a star above each of them.

I thought a few of the details would help create the mood, so I put two stars above them. For example, I wanted to create a feeling of danger in the story—I'm always nervous that Haskell will fall and get hurt on the playground—so I starred the detail about the kids crying. I thought it would suggest this mood.

Coach the Student

I'd like to help you talk this strategy out before you try it in your writer's notebook.

▶ Let's start with "sight." Close your eyes and try to "see" your setting. What do you "see"?

▶ Which of these details will best help readers "see" the setting?

- Great. Now let's focus on the other senses. What do you "hear"? "Smell"? What can you "feel"? "Taste"?
- Which details will help you create the mood of the story?

Link to the Student's Writing

I'd like you to try the "five senses" strategy in your writer's notebook. Use all five senses to think of more details for this setting. Then reread the details you come up with, and think about which ones will make a good backdrop. Think also about which setting details will help you create the mood you want in your story.

Keep in mind that writers have to work hard to think of setting details for their stories. Using the "five senses" strategy is one way to do this work.

FOLLOW-UP

▶ In future conferences, offer additional strategies for imagining a setting before drafting. One strategy is to sketch the setting in the writer's notebook. Another is to draw a floor plan of a room or a map of the area where the story takes place.

▶ Many students need help applying the setting details in their drafts. In Book 2: *Drafts,* two conferences can help: Conference 17, "Crafting a Lead by Describing the Setting," and Conference 26, "Crafting a Scene by Weaving in Setting Details."

SOURCES

Ralph Fletcher's writing about setting in *What a Writer Needs* (1993)—one of the most important books written about teaching the craft—is the inspiration for this conference.

SIGHT: Bright blue sky, brilliant sunshine.
Monkey bars, slides, sandboxes. Hundreds of
children scampering around, climbing equipment.
Parents, some following their children, others
sitting on benches talking to other parents.
Empty strollers everywhere. Some kids on top
of monkey bars, twenty feet off the ground.

SOUND: Tree leaves rustling. Lawnmowers buzzing.
Kids shrieking in excitement. A few kids crying
from some minor scrapes. Parents telling kids
to be careful.

SMELL: Freshly cut grass. Pretzels roasting in
food carts. Old diapers in garbage cans.

TOUCH: Warm breeze on my face. Warm,
smooth metal (when I climb the monkey
bars behind Haskell).

TASTE: Salty pretzel and delicious strawberry
when I eat snacks with Haskell.

© 2009 by Carl Anderson from *Strategic Writing Conferences* (Portsmouth, NH: Heinemann). This page may be reproduced for classroom use only.

22

Developing a Nonfiction Topic by Finding a Focus

WHAT YOU FIND

The student who could be helped by this conference

- has written generalized entries about a topic ("all about" entries).
- is unsure how to begin developing her topic in her writer's notebook.
- may not see that there are many possibilities for a focus that are already embedded in her writing.

CONFERENCE PURPOSE

Teach the student to find a single focus for the non-fiction topic she is writing about.

MODEL TEXTS

"Cat Talk" by D.S. Long

My writer's notebook entry or another writer's notebook entry in which the writer brainstorms focus possibilities for a nonfiction piece

◆ It isn't necessary to use D.S. Long's "Cat Talk" in this conference. Use a feature article from your collection or from magazines such as *Boys' Life* or *TIME For Kids*.

I CAN SEE THAT YOU'VE picked a really interesting topic for a feature article. As I look through your notebook, I see that you've written a few entries about a whole bunch of things you know about the topic.

When writers write a feature article, they don't usually write "all about" the topic. Instead, they focus on one aspect, or part, of the topic. Feature article writers call the aspect of the topic they focus on their "angle." I want to teach you how to find an angle for your article.

Share Model Texts

In each feature article we have read, the writer has had an angle on his or her topic. For example, in "Cat Talk," we learned about the ways cats communicate. The angle author D.S. Long takes on the topic of cats is how cats "talk." The whole article is about this angle. There isn't a section on different kinds of cats, or on foods cats eat, or on reasons cats make great pets. That's because these aspects about cats don't fit with the author's chosen angle.

Share Your Writing

How do we find an angle—one specific idea—to focus on for their draft? We ask ourselves, "What aspects of this topic am I interested in writing about?" To answer this question, we read all our entries in our writer's notebook about the topic. Or we think about the topic and everything we know about it. As we come up with possible angles, we make a list of them in our writer's notebook. Then we choose just one of these angles to write about.

The Beatles:

- the instruments they played
- (their number one songs)
- their albums
- What was "Beatlemania"?
- their movies
- why the band broke up in 1970

I used this strategy when I decided to write a feature article about the Beatles, one of the best rock 'n' roll bands ever. As I considered all that I knew about them, I asked myself, "What aspects of this topic am I interested in writing about?" I made a list of the possible angles in my notebook.

After I brainstormed these possible angles, I had to decide which one I wanted to write about in my article. I picked "Their Number One Songs" and, as you can see, I circled it on my list. I really love these songs and wanted to share what I know about a few of them in an article. In this way, I could introduce the band to people who don't know that much about them.

Coach the Student

I want to help you find one part of your topic to focus on for your draft.

▶ Reread the entries you wrote about your topic. As you read, ask yourself, "What aspects of this topic am I interested in writing about?"

▶ Think about your topic. Ask yourself, "What angles could I take on my topic?"

Link to the Student's Writing

I'd like you to continue brainstorming possible angles for your feature article. Then take some time to decide on one angle you're going to write about. Remember that when writers write nonfiction, like in a feature article, they choose one part of their topic to focus on.

MODIFICATIONS FOR NONFICTION GENRES

▶ *Op-Ed*
If the student is writing an op-ed, say, "I want to help you think about the opinions you have about your topic. Start by rereading the entries you wrote about your topic. As you read, ask yourself, 'What opinions do I have about this topic? Which one am I interested in writing about?' "

▶ *Personal Essay*
If the student is writing a personal essay, say, "I want to help you think about the ideas you have for your topic. Reread your entries about the topic. As you read, ask yourself, 'What ideas about this topic am I interested in writing about?' "

SOURCES

Randy Bomer's course in nonfiction writing at the Teachers College Reading and Writing Project (TCRWP) 1993 Summer Institute was the original inspiration for this conference. He also writes about it in *Time for Meaning: Crafting Literate Lives in Middle & High School* (1995).

The Beatles:

- the instruments they played
- their number one songs
- their albums
- What was "Beatlemania"?
- their movies
- why the band broke up in 1970

© 2009 by Carl Anderson from *Strategic Writing Conferences* (Portsmouth, NH: Heinemann). This page may be reproduced for classroom use only.

23

Developing a Nonfiction Topic by Brainstorming Sections

WHAT YOU FIND

The student who could be helped by this conference has chosen a focus for her writing but still needs to:

- generate ideas for sections.
- gather details in order to write a well-developed draft.

CONFERENCE PURPOSE

Teach the student to brainstorm sections for a nonfiction piece and to gather the information she already knows for each section.

MODEL TEXT

My writer's notebook entry or another writer's notebook entry that lists sections for a nonfiction draft

◆ The approach of this conference about writing sections is different than the one usually taken by the teachers we had as kids. Teachers often asked us to gather lots of facts first, then organize them into categories or sections. Consequently, many of us, unsure of which facts were important, gathered way more than we needed.

By teaching students to brainstorm possible subtopics *before* they start gathering facts about their topic, we give them a way to determine which facts are important, and are worthy of being copied down—and which ones aren't. Of course, we need to be open to the possibility that as students gather facts, they might revise their list of subtopics to better fit their material.

I SEE THAT YOU HAVE a focus for your nonfiction topic. The next step is to figure out what the different parts of your piece could be. We have read a whole bunch of feature articles in this unit of study. One thing we noticed about feature articles is that they have several sections. Why did the feature writers create sections? Writers divide their articles into parts in order to organize all the information they gathered. The "chunks" help readers make sense of all the information. Information that is connected in one way goes in one section, information that is connected in another way goes in another section. One thing we do before we write an article is to brainstorm a list of the possible sections.

Another thing we noticed about feature articles is that there are several facts in each section. To have facts in each section, we gather them before we draft. Our notebook is a great place to organize our thinking about the different parts of our article and to gather the facts, the information we will write about in each section of our draft.

We can use our writer's notebook as a tool to help us figure out the sections of our feature article. When we know the sections, we can figure out the information we need to gather to write each section. Then we will have a better idea of the facts we should write down in our notebook—we write down the facts connected to the sections.

Share Your Writing

Take a look inside my writer's notebook, where I gathered and organized the information I needed to write a feature article. The

◆ To be able to break down a topic into sections (subtopics) and then brainstorm facts about each section, students have to be familiar with the topic. This conference is designed for a student who is writing about a topic he or she *already* knows a lot about. If students are about to gather information about a topic that they are unfamiliar with, have Book 1: *Topics*, Conference 25, "Developing an Unfamiliar Nonfiction Topic by Researching Sections," with them instead.

topic I was interested in writing about was hermit crabs, and my focus was how to care for them.

First, I brainstormed possible sections for my article.

Hermit Crabs

- What kinds of food they eat
- Keeping hermit crabs at the right temperature
- Kinds of equipment hermit crabs need

To come up with these sections, I asked myself, "What are some of the things I know about my focus?" As I thought about it, I realized that I know about the food that hermit crabs eat, how to keep them warm, and the kinds of equipment they need in their cage. I wrote them as a list. Then, at the top of the next page of my notebook, I wrote the name of a section.

I wrote the rest of the section names at the top of the next few pages.

What Kinds of Food They Eat

- they eat almost anything
- meat, fish, vegetables, and fruit
- oak leaves and tree bark

    [dry the leaves - crabs like them CRUNCHY!]

- dried organic marigold petals

    [organic - grown without pesticides]

Keeping Hermit Crabs at the Right Temperature

- temperature no lower than 72°F

    [lower temperatures kill crabs - so do higher temperatures, from sitting in sunlight]

- need an under-tank heater
- 70% humidity - want a moist, tropical "feel"

> Kinds of Equipment Hermit Crabs Need
>
> - 10 gallon glass aquarium
> - sand and coconut fiber
> - water dish
>   [not too deep - smaller crabs will drown!]
> - toys - choya wood
>   - driftwood
>   - coral
>   - "hermie huts"
>   - clay flower pots

I was ready to start gathering facts that I already knew. I needed to write down facts about each of the sections of my topic. To write facts on each page, I asked myself, "What do I know about *this* section?" As facts came to mind, I jotted them down. Only after I did all this work was I really ready to write my feature article—because I knew what my sections were going to be, and I had several interesting facts to write about in each section.

Coach the Student

Now it's time for you to get ready to write a feature article using this strategy.

▶ First, what's your focus?

▶ Tell me some of the sections you think your article could have. Ask yourself, "What are some of the things I know about my focus?"

▶ That's a good start. Turn to the next page of your notebook and, at the top, write "Possible Sections."

▶ List the ideas for sections that you just told me about and any others you can think of.

▶ Write the name of each section at the top of a page so that you have a whole page to work with for each section. Then you can write down facts on each page that go with the section.

Link to the Student's Writing

Now it's time for you to start using your writer's notebook to brainstorm the sections and to gather the information you need to write the sections. The important thing to remember is that when you write a nonfiction draft, it often helps to think of sections first, then list the information that goes with each section. Your writer's notebook is a great place to do this important work.

MODIFICATIONS FOR NONFICTION GENRES

For students to be able to brainstorm sections and gather information for them independently, they usually need several guided experiences. Have this conference with students again, when they are writing in other nonfiction genres, to help them gain a basic understanding of how to use this strategy.

▶ *Op-Ed*

If students are writing op-eds, explain that they are going to brainstorm the reasons (sections) for their opinion, what they believe will persuade readers to think as they do. Also, explain that they will need to gather evidence to support each reason—facts, personal experiences, and quotes from experts gathered from interviews.

▶ *Personal Essay*

If students are writing personal essays, explain that they are going to brainstorm the reasons (sections) that will help readers understand their idea (thesis). Also explain that they will gather life stories to support each reason.

Hermit Crabs

- What kinds of food they eat
- Keeping hermit crabs at the right temperature
- Kinds of equipment hermit crabs need

© 2009 by Carl Anderson from *Strategic Writing Conferences* (Portsmouth, NH: Heinemann). This page may be reproduced for classroom use only.

What Kinds of Food They Eat

- they eat almost anything

- meat, fish, vegetables, and fruit

- oak leaves and tree bark

  [dry the leaves - crabs like them CRUNCHY!]

- dried organic marigold petals

  [organic - grown without pesticides]

© 2009 by Carl Anderson from *Strategic Writing Conferences* (Portsmouth, NH: Heinemann). This page may be reproduced for classroom use only.

Keeping Hermit Crabs at the Right Temperature

- temperature no lower than 72°F

  [lower temperatures kill crabs - so
    do higher temperatures, from sitting
    in sunlight]

- need an under - tank heater

- 70% humidity - want a moist, tropical "feel"

© 2009 by Carl Anderson from *Strategic Writing Conferences* (Portsmouth, NH: Heinemann). This page may be reproduced for classroom use only.

Kinds of Equipment Hermit Crabs Need

- 10 gallon glass acqvarium

- sand and coconut fiber

- water dish

[not too deep - smaller crabs will drown!]

- toys - choya wood
        - driftwood
        - coral
        - " hermit huts "
        - clay flower pots

© 2009 by Carl Anderson from *Strategic Writing Conferences* (Portsmouth, NH: Heinemann). This page may be reproduced for classroom use only.

24

Developing an Unfamiliar Nonfiction Topic by Finding a Focus

WHAT YOU FIND

The student who could be helped by this conference:

- has chosen or has been assigned an unfamiliar topic for his piece.
- is researching the topic, but hasn't yet figured out what aspect to focus on.
- has notes on facts that pertain to many aspects of the topic.
- has decided on an angle or thesis topic and has taken notes about facts that are interesting—but that don't correspond to his angle.

CONFERENCE PURPOSE

Teach the student to find a focus for researching a nonfiction topic he doesn't know a lot about as a precursor to writing a draft.

MODEL TEXT

My writer's notebook entry or another writer's notebook entry that lists possible angles for a nonfiction draft

◆ Writers sometimes write nonfiction pieces about topics they initially know very little about. One of their challenges is to figure out the aspect of the topic they want to focus on. Without a focus in mind, writers would be unable to decide which facts they will note, and which they will not.

◆ Because it's challenging for students to find a focus for reseaching an unfamiliar topic, it's tempting to give them one. When we do this for them, students miss the opportunity to learn how to do this themselves.

You have chosen your topic and are doing research to learn more about it. Great work! I want you to know that learning about a new topic, and then writing about it, is a *big* challenge for a feature article writer. I see you have notes on all sorts of interesting things that relate to your topic, but you haven't found your focus yet. The challenge is to figure out what *one part* of the topic to focus on in the article—what angle to take on the topic.

When we write about an unfamiliar topic, we have to get an overview of the topic *as a whole* before we can figure out which part to focus on. This involves doing a special kind of reading. First, we find sources that give an overview of the topic—encyclopedia entries, textbooks, a book or article that surveys the topic, an exhibit in a museum, a video. These sources tell us a little bit about many parts of the topic. They don't usually go into great detail, but they are great for giving us ideas for finding a focus.

Then we read to learn about the aspects of the topic. Sometimes this reading involves skimming the whole book, article, or entry. Sometimes it means piecing together information from different parts of a text, like from a table of contents or chapter titles. Other times this reading involves subheadings of an article or encyclopedia entry. And sometimes it involves a close reading of the source material.

As we do this kind of reading, we gain a general knowledge of the whole topic. And, hopefully, we also get excited about one aspect of the topic. We make that aspect the focus of our draft because we want to share our new knowledge and excitement with readers.

◆ You could also have this conference with students who are writing reports, profiles, or biographies—any genre that informs readers about a topic.

The Wright brothers:

- What is "three-axis control"?
- Who were the Wright brothers' competitors?
- How did the Wright brothers use what they knew about bicycles when they designed airplanes?

Share Your Writing

I decided to write a feature article on the Wright Brothers, a topic that I was curious about. I didn't know much about them at first, except for the fact that they were the first people to successfully fly an airplane. I knew that before I took any notes in my writer's notebook about them, I had to learn more about the whole topic of the Wright Brothers and then decide the one angle I wanted to write about.

The first thing I did was find a source that gave an overview of the Wright Brothers. I looked online at an encyclopedia and found a long entry on them. Then, before I started reading the entry, I created a special page in my writer's notebook that I titled, "The Wright Brothers".

As I read the encyclopedia entry, I made a list of possible angles I could focus on for further research. How did I come up with these angles? As I read the encyclopedia entry, I learned various things about the Wright Brothers, some of which interested me, some of which didn't. I wrote down the things that interested me. For example, I learned that the Wright Brothers invented something called "three-axis control," a way to steer airplanes that is still used today. I thought this sounded interesting to learn about, so I jotted it down on my "Possible Angles" page. A little further along in the entry, I read that other people claimed that they were the first to build and fly an airplane. This caught my eye, so I wrote it down as a possible angle, too. I continued to read, and several pages later, I learned something that really caught my eye—the Wright Brothers owned a bicycle shop, and they used what they knew about bicycles to help them design their airplane. So I jotted this down on my "Possible Angles" page.

Once I made my list, I read it over and selected one angle: how the Wright Brothers used what they knew about bicycles to help them design airplanes. Once I chose this part of the topic to focus on, I was ready to do more research and start taking notes—notes *only* about how owning a bicycle shop helped the Wright Brothers design their airplane. Coming up with the angle helped me do research that was focused on just one aspect of the Wright Brothers. That sure saved me a lot of time—and work—because I only needed to read and take notes about my focus, not about everything else.

Coach the Student

I'd like to help you find an angle to take for your topic research—and ultimately for your draft.

❱ What topic are you interested in writing about?

❱ What source would give you a general overview about this topic?

❱ Start a list in your writer's notebook of possible angles to focus on. Let's start by skimming the table of contents and subheadings of your source. Are there any specific aspects of your topic that catch your attention?

❱ As you discover interesting things that you might want to focus on, add them to your list of possible angles.

◆ Be prepared to suggest a source that gives an overview of a topic—for example, an encyclopedia entry—or to suggest where the student could find such a source.

Link to the Student's Writing

I'd like you to keep reading and see if you can identify several possible angles. Remember, when we are getting ready to write about a topic that we are interested in or curious about, our first challenge is to learn more about the parts of the topic. Then we figure out what to focus on. In the initial stages of research, we read to identify focus possibilities, select one, and then gather information about that focus before we draft.

FOLLOW-UP

There are two general approaches to take with students once they've identified a focus. In one, students read about their focus and take notes as they read; later on, they sort their notes into categories that become the sections of their piece.

In the second approach, students read about their focus and identify possible subtopics before they start taking notes. They can then devote a page (or several pages) to each subtopic. As they read and encounter a fact they want to record, they can write it on the corresponding page in their notebook. (This approach is the focus of Book 1: *Topics*, Conference 25, "Developing an Unfamiliar Nonfiction Topic by Researching Sections.")

Although you will probably address one (or both) of these approaches in minilessons, it's likely that you will need to confer with students about the information-gathering phase of their research, too.

The Wright brothers:

- What is "three-axis control"?
- Who were the Wright brothers' competitors?
- How did the Wright brothers use what they knew about bicycles when they designed airplanes?

© 2009 by Carl Anderson from *Strategic Writing Conferences* (Portsmouth, NH: Heinemann). This page may be reproduced for classroom use only.

25

Developing an Unfamiliar Nonfiction Topic by Researching Sections

WHAT YOU FIND

The student who could be helped by this conference has researched an unfamiliar topic and has decided which angle to take on it for her written piece, but she may:

- be unsure what the sections of the written piece will be.
- be having trouble determining what notes to write down as she researches.
- be writing down almost everything she learns.
- not know how to determine which information is important for her purpose, and which information is not.

CONFERENCE PURPOSE

Teach the student to determine the sections of a nonfiction piece while researching an unfamiliar topic.

MODEL TEXT

My writer's notebook entry or another writer's notebook entry that lists sections for a nonfiction draft

◆ It can be a challenge for students to figure out the angle to take and the sections of their written piece. Having a sense of the points they want to make helps them determine which information to note as they research, and which to ignore.

Writers often make an initial guess about the sections/points of interest at the beginning of their research. They do this by skimming research sources, especially sources that provide an overview of the topic. Although writers may rethink the points they want to make as they research, the initial guess gives them a framework for determining which information to record.

I'M GLAD THAT YOU ARE interested in learning about this topic for your feature article. And it's great that you've figured out what angle to take when you write your draft. Knowing your focus helps when you're researching a topic you don't initially know much about.

It can be challenging to figure out what the sections of a piece are going to be when we're researching and writing about a new topic. Figuring out what the sections will be makes gathering facts much easier. I want to teach you a strategy for doing this important work.

Explain a Strategy

We *could* gather a lot of facts in our writer's notebook about the topic and then figure out what categories all the facts fit into once we are finished. That's one way of figuring out what the sections of the written piece will be. But this is an inefficient way of conducting research. When we gather facts this way, we often take way too many notes—because how do we know which facts to note and which to exclude?

There is another strategy we can use to organize our thinking and writing. Before we start taking notes, we can make an educated guess about what the sections of our written piece will be. This way, as we research, we at least have a sense of what we might need. We look for facts that we could include in each section. As we research, we might realize that we need to revise the initial list of sections— that sometimes happens as we learn about an unfamiliar topic—but at least we have a direction when we start out.

◆ For this conference to be successful, students must have sources that they can read. It's helpful for students to have sources that give an overview of their topic, such as encyclopedia entries or general books. With these sources, students are better able to identify ways for breaking their topic into sections.

How do we make an educated guess about what the sections will be? One strategy is to skim though our sources—encyclopedia entries, articles, books—and see how the authors categorized their information. We skim, looking at the subheadings of an encyclopedia entry or article, or we look at the table of contents of a book. Or we read the topic sentences in an article or chapter. This gives us ideas for what the subheadings might be.

Share Your Writing

I was planning to write an article about ancient Greece, and I decided that I wanted to focus my piece on some of the famous buildings that the ancient Greeks built. To help me figure out what my sections might be, I skimmed through an encyclopedia entry about the architecture of ancient Greece. Here is the encyclopedia article I used. I noticed that one of the subheadings was about the Parthenon, a famous temple in Athens. So I wrote this on my list of possible sections.

I continued to skim through the encyclopedia entry, and saw another subheading, about the Oracle at Delphi. The Oracle at Delphi was where the ancient Greeks went in hope that they would learn about their future. I wrote it on my list of possible sections. I continued to read through the encyclopedia entry, and got ideas for several other sections.

Once I came up with several possible sections, I began to read and take notes on the different buildings on the list. As I researched, I did make a few changes to my list. For example, in other sources, I read about some buildings that weren't discussed in the encyclopedia entry, and I added them to my list. Also, I crossed off the list one of the buildings after I realized that it wasn't one of the most important ones.

Famous Buildings of Ancient Greece

- the Parthenon
- the Oracle at Delphi
- the Temple of Poseidon
- Olympia
- the Temple of Zeus
- the Athenian Agora

Coach the Student

I'd like to help you get started thinking about what your sections might be. Could you take out one of the sources you're going to use for your research?

If the student's source is an encyclopedia entry or article:

▶ I'd like you to skim through the source and look at the headings. Could any of these headings be sections in your article?

◆ Some students need more guidance than others in reading through their sources. You may need to model how to identify a possible section. Demonstrate with students' sources and then give them the opportunity to identify a possible section.

If the student's source is a book:

▶ I'd like you to skim through the table of contents. Could any of the chapter titles work as sections in your article?

If the student's source [an article or chapter in a book] doesn't have headings:

▶ I'd like you to skim through the source and read topic sentences. As you read, look for ideas for sections.

Link to the Student's Writing

I'd like for you to continue brainstorming possible sections on your own now. Once you've come up with several, you'll be ready to start reading and taking notes. You want to look for facts that will fit into these sections. For each section, you can devote a page or two in your notebook for notes. Be open to the idea that as you learn about your topic, you might get ideas for new sections. Or you may decide that you don't really need one of the sections on your original list.

Remember that when writers research an unfamiliar topic, they often make an educated guess about what the sections of their written piece will be. Having a sense of what their sections will be helps them figure out which facts to write down as notes.

Famous Buildings of Ancient Greece

- the Parthenon
- the Oracle at Delphi
- the Temple of Poseidon
- Olympia
- the Temple of Zeus
- the Athenian Agora

© 2009 by Carl Anderson from *Strategic Writing Conferences* (Portsmouth, NH: Heinemann). This page may be reproduced for classroom use only.

26

Developing a Nonfiction Topic by Making a Resource List

WHAT YOU FIND

The student who could be helped by this conference:

- feels frustrated because he isn't sure how to find the information he needs to write a piece.
- has found one resource for his research—typically a website or an online encyclopedia—and is over-relying on it.

CONFERENCE PURPOSE

Teach the student to make a resource list for gathering information that will help him write a well-developed nonfiction piece.

MODEL TEXT

My writer's notebook entry or another writer's notebook entry that contains a resource list

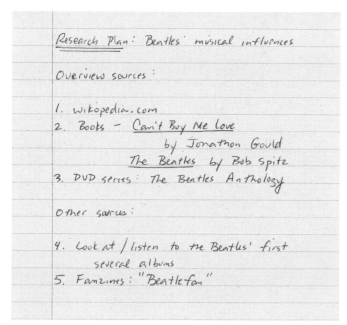

I SEE THAT YOU'RE NOT sure where you can get the information you need to write a well-developed nonfiction piece about your topic. It's quite common for writers to feel a bit lost, even overwhelmed, when they start researching a topic. They wonder where on earth they are going to learn enough to write their piece. To use our precious time well, we can make a *resource list*—a list of resources we will use to get the information we need. With a resource list in hand, we have a road map to guide us in our research. I want to teach you how to make a resource list.

Share Your Writing

I'm going to show you a resource list I made in my writer's notebook about a topic I wanted to write a feature article about.

I wanted to write an article on the musicians who influenced the Beatles, such as Elvis Presley, a topic that I didn't know much about. I made this list of possible resources that I thought could give me the information I needed. One thing that I've found important is to start with resources that give a general overview of my topic—so you can see that the first resource on my list is www.wikipedia.com.

Another thing I've found helpful when gathering nonfiction information is to include a variety of resources. I included several kinds of resources that I thought could give information on my topic, such as books, specialty magazine articles, music magazines and fanzines, video/DVD documentaries, and even some Beatles CDs.

Having a list like this helped me when I went to the library to do research. I looked immediately for books on the Beatles. And I looked at music magazines, too. Having a list helped me search online for resources. When I searched online using Google, I tried keywords such as "Beatles DVDs" and "Beatles fanzines."

To help you think about all the different resources you might use in your research, I'm giving you a resource list (page 140) that you can tape into your writer's notebook.

Coach the Student

I'd like to help you begin to think out your research list for your topic. Take a moment to look at the resource list I gave you.

▶ As you read, ask yourself which resources might have good information about your topic.

▶ Which resources do you think you'll include on your list?

Link to the Student's Writing

I'd like you to do some more thinking about your resource list on your own now, and write the list in your writer's notebook, just like I did. Once you've done that, you can start looking for resources.

Remember that sometimes when you write, you're going to need to find information about the topic you're going to write about— and that making a resource list makes it easier for you to find the information you need in order to write well about your topic.

FOLLOW-UP

Another time to have this conference with students is when they are drafting or revising a piece and have discovered that there are gaps in what they know about their topic. Writers sometimes have to take time out from drafting or revising to do research to fill in gaps.

Research Plan: Beatles' musical influences

Overview sources:

1. wikopedia.com
2. Books — <u>Can't Buy Me Love</u>
                    by Jonathon Gould
              <u>The Beatles</u> by Bob Spitz
3. DVD series: The Beatles Anthology

Other sorces:

4. Look at / listen to the Beatles' first
        several albums
5. Fanzines: "Beatlefan"

© 2009 by Carl Anderson from *Strategic Writing Conferences* (Portsmouth, NH: Heinemann). This page may be reproduced for classroom use only.

Resource List

◗ Get an overview of the topic by reading an encyclopedia or textbook entry.

◗ Read books about the topic, including picture books.

◗ Visit websites, view podcasts, and read blogs about the topic.

◗ Read magazines or "fanzines" about the topic.

◗ Watch videos about the topic.

◗ Talk to experts on the topic.

◗ Visit museums or zoos with exhibits devoted to the topic.

◗ Attend presentations or conventions on the topic.

◗ Experience the topic directly. (For example, if the topic is music, attend concerts; if the topic is baseball, attend baseball games.)

◗ Attend presentations or conventions that focus on the topic.

© 2009 by Carl Anderson from *Strategic Writing Conferences* (Portsmouth, NH: Heinemann). This page may be reproduced for classroom use only.

27

Developing a Nonfiction Topic by Gathering Notes

WHAT YOU FIND

The student who could be helped by this conference is researching and taking notes on the topic he is going to write about but is:

- overwhelmed and frustrated by the task.
- bored by the process.
- copying source material word-for-word in his writer's notebook.

CONFERENCE PURPOSE

Teach the student to take notes about the topic he is developing for a nonfiction piece.

MODEL TEXTS

"Cape Cod Whale Watching," an excerpt from *Cape Cod Guide* (published by Meds Maps)

My writer's notebook entry or another writer's notebook entry of notes about a nonfiction topic

◆ Some students copy from a source because they're having trouble reading it. Consequently, they find it difficult to decide what is important to write down. Help students find a source they can easily read before you have this conference.

You know a lot about the research process. I see you came up with an angle for writing about your topic, that you've been figuring out what the sections of your article will be, that you've set up your notebook to gather the facts you need to write these sections. You have also found sources for getting facts about your topic. These are all important steps writers make when they're developing a nonfiction topic.

However, I'm noticing that in your notes about the topic, you are copying words, sentences, even whole paragraphs from the source. I want to teach you how to take notes about your topic instead of copying from a source.

Think ahead a moment. In a few days, you're going to be writing a draft about your topic. When readers read that draft, it should sound like *you* wrote it. When we copy what another author has written about our topic word-for-word in our writer's notebook, it's all too easy to take what we have copied and put it right into our draft. Then we have written a draft that doesn't sound like us at all—because another author actually wrote the words. Also, when a writer copies what another writer wrote, it is considered stealing. This kind of stealing has a special name: *plagiarism.*

Explain a Strategy

Instead of copying word-for-word from a source, we take notes. As we read about a topic, we ask, "What is important to remember about what I just read?" How do we decide what is important to remember? If a fact is connected to the aspect of the topic we are researching—our focus, or angle—then it's important.

When we decide that something we read is important, we jot down just a few key words, or sometimes a few phrases or sentences, about what we read to help us remember what we have learned. And because we only write down the key things to remember, when we turn our notes into the sections of our draft, we write our own sentences, in our individual style, with our individual voice.

Share Your Writing

I want to show you the notes I took when I was researching whale behaviors for an article. First, let me read you the passage about breaching that I read from a book on whales called *Cape Cod Whale Watching*.

> Many species of whales, dolphins, and porpoises can be seen leaping clear out of the water, a behavior known as breaching. When a whale breaches, it dives for a few minutes, then hurls itself upward with all its might, breaks the surface like a rocket, soars straight up as high as it can, and lands on its side or back with a tremendous splash.
>
> Breaching is a spectacular act that never fails to impress people fortunate enough to see it. There are many theories about its function. Breaching may serve as a means of communication. The loud splash made by a belly-flopping whale can be heard for great distances underwater, where sound travels more readily than in air. By breaching, a whale may make its presence known to another individual quite far away.

After I read this passage and was taking notes, I asked myself the important question, "What is important to remember about what I just read?" This helped me decide which facts to write down in my notebook.

Sometimes I encounter an important fact in a sentence, and I jot down a few words about it. For example, after I read the first sentence, I felt I learned something I didn't know about whales, which was that they do something called *breaching*. So I jotted down a few key words about what I had read—the name of the behavior,

Cape Cod Whale Watching
Section, "Breaching" (no page number)

- Whales "breach," or leap out of the water

- Whales dive first, then move straight up, travel up into the air, then land with a giant splash

- breaching may be communication. The sound of the splash tells other whales he/she's there

and its definition—instead of copying the entire sentence. See, I jotted down, "Whales *breach*, or leap out of the water."

Often, I wait to take notes until after I've read a whole paragraph or whole section. Then I synthesize what I've read by writing a sentence or two about it in my notes. For example, after I read the second paragraph of this passage, I asked myself, "What is important to remember about what I just read?" I wrote down just this: "Breaching may be communication. The sound of the splash tells other whales that he/she's there."

Coach the Student

I'd like to help you take notes from your source.

▶ Read the first couple of sentences of your source aloud.

▶ What is important to remember about what you just read? Good. You didn't retell every word the author said; you came up with just a few words to help you remember what you read.

▶ Now try it again. Read the next few sentences aloud. What is important to remember about what you just read? Sometimes it helps to look away from the text when you are trying to decide what notes to take.

Link to the Student's Writing

I can tell you are ready to try this on your own. Remember that writers don't copy everything they read when they do research. They take notes by thinking about what they have read and deciding what is most important to jot down.

FOLLOW-UP

▶ Some students take way too many notes from a source, jotting down key words about every sentence that they read. Suggest that students skim the source first to get a sense of what is most important before they start to take notes.

▶ There are other strategies to teach students that help them write nonfiction in their own voice. One strategy is to ask students to periodically talk with a partner or a small group about the information they are learning about their topic as research. Suggest that they discuss their research every day during the share session at the end of writing workshop. By talking about the facts and their questions, students discover their own way of communicating the new information they have learned. Another strategy is to teach students to read over their notes before drafting a section, *close their notebooks*, and then write the section without looking at their notes.

Cape Cod Whale Watching

Many species of whales, dolphins, and porpoises can be seen leaping clear out of the water, a behavior known as breaching. When a whale breaches, it dives for a few minutes, then hurls itself upward with all its might, breaks the surface like a rocket, soars straight up as high as it can, and lands on its side or back with a tremendous splash.

Breaching is a spectacular act that never fails to impress people fortunate enough to see it. There are many theories about its function. Breaching may serve as a means of communication. The loud splash made by a belly-flopping whale can be heard for great distances underwater, where sound travels more readily than in air. By breaching, a whale may make its presence known to another individual quite far away.

– from "Cape Cod Whale Watching,"
from Meds Maps (from *Cape Cod Guide*)

© 2009 by Carl Anderson from *Strategic Writing Conferences* (Portsmouth, NH: Heinemann). This page may be reproduced for classroom use only.

© 2009 by Carl Anderson from *Strategic Writing Conferences* (Portsmouth, NH: Heinemann). This page may be reproduced for classroom use only.

Cape Cod Whale Watching
Section, "Breaching" (no page number)

- Whales "breach," or leap out of the water

- Whales dive first, then move straight up, travel up into the air, then land with a giant splash

- breaching may be communication. The sound of the splash tells other whales he/she's there

28

Developing a Nonfiction Topic by Preparing to Interview

WHAT YOU FIND

The student who could be helped by this conference plans to do an interview as part of her research on a topic but:

- has not done any preparation for the interview.
- has brainstormed only a few interview questions—and the questions won't lead to in-depth information.

CONFERENCE PURPOSE

Teach the student to prepare to conduct an interview about her topic by writing open-ended questions.

MODEL TEXT

My writer's notebook entry or another writer's notebook entry of interview questions

I'M EXCITED THAT you want to conduct an interview to research your topic. Writers usually do a lot of preparation before conducting an interview. That's what I want to talk with you about today.

What does it mean to prepare for an interview? Writers think hard about the questions that they want to ask *ahead of time*. They often start the interview with a list in hand of the questions they want to ask. This makes it more likely that they'll get the information they want.

Explain a Strategy

There are a couple of things we need to consider when preparing for an interview.

First, where are we going to make notes as we prepare? Our writer's notebook is a good place to list the questions we might ask. It is also a good place to take notes while conducting the interview.

Second, we want to think very carefully about the questions we are going to ask. How do we come up with these questions? One way is to think about the sections that we plan to write about, and then write questions that will produce information about those sections. For example, if we are planning to write a feature article about snowboarding tricks and one of our sections is "The McTwist," then we might want to ask the question, "Could you tell me the secrets of doing a good McTwist?"

And, third, we want to ask *open-ended questions*; that is, questions that invite someone to respond with more than a yes/no answer. Instead of asking, "Do you like doing the McTwist?", which can be answered with a simple yes or no, we ask, "How do you do a McTwist?" or "Why do you like to do the McTwist?" These questions can elicit a more detailed response. To write an open-ended question, we start it with *who, what, where, why,* or *how.*

Share Your Writing

I want you to take a look at the work I did in my writer's notebook to prepare for an interview with a veterinarian. I was doing research for a feature article on taking care of cats. Do you see how I brainstormed my sections on this first page?

> "Taking Care of Cats"
>
> - Cat food
> - Cat exercise
> - the litter box
> - Cat toys

Then on the next page, I brainstormed some of the questions I could ask the veterinarian about the sections.

> Interview Questions
>
> - What are the best kinds of food to feed cats?
> - What are the best brands of cat food?
> - What kinds of things can cat owners do to help their cats get enough exercise?
> - Where is the best place to put the cat litter box?
> - What are the best brands of cat litter?
> - What kinds of toys do cats like?

Since the first section I wanted to include in the article was "Cat Food," I came up with the *what* question, "What are the best kinds of food to feed cats?"

Another section was "Cat Exercise," so I came up with another *what* question: "What kinds of things can cat owners do to help their cats get enough exercise?"

And, since I thought I might have a section called "The Cat Litter Box," I thought I would ask the vet the *where* question, "Where is the best place to put the cat litter box?"

Coach the Student

I'd like to help you brainstorm questions you might ask in the interview about your topic.

▶ What kinds of *who*, *what*, *where*, *why*, or *how* questions do you want to ask about your first section?

▶ If any of those questions have simple answers that aren't that helpful or interesting, then don't write them down. Sometimes questions that get answered yes or no are not worth asking.

▶ What about your second section? What kinds of *who*, *what*, *where*, *why*, or *how* questions do you want to ask?

Link to the Student's Writing

I think you're off to a good start brainstorming interview questions. I'd like you to spend some time brainstorming more questions now, jotting them down in your writer's notebook.

Keep in mind that for an interview to be successful, writers prepare for it beforehand. *Before* starting, they think of questions that are likely to reveal interesting thinking and facts about their topic. Thoughtful, open-ended questions often lead to fascinating answers.

FOLLOW-UP

One aspect of interviewing is how to ask follow-up questions. Students who are new to interviewing usually conduct interviews by asking their questions one after another, without stopping to ask follow-up questions.

Unless you're with students as they interview their subject, it can be difficult to teach them how to ask follow-up questions. One way to teach this is to have students review the notes they took during their interview to find things they would like to ask the person they interviewed more about. You can suggest that students conduct a second interview with their subject to ask these follow-up questions—and suggest that as they talk with the subject the second time, they ask follow-up questions whenever their curiosity is piqued *during* the interview.

"Taking Care of Cats"

- Cat food
- Cat exercise
- the litter box
- Cat toys

© 2009 by Carl Anderson from *Strategic Writing Conferences* (Portsmouth, NH: Heinemann). This page may be reproduced for classroom use only.

Interview Questions

- What are the best kinds of food to feed cats?
- What are the best brands of cat food?
- What kinds of things can cat owners do to help their cats get enough exercise?
- Where is the best place to put the cat litter box?
- What are the best brands of cat litter?
- What kinds of toys do cats like?

© 2009 by Carl Anderson from *Strategic Writing Conferences* (Portsmouth, NH: Heinemann). This page may be reproduced for classroom use only.

29

Preparing to Draft by Making a Plan

WHAT YOU FIND

The student who could be helped by this conference has a seed topic and may have tried a few strategies to develop the topic but:

- says he will think of more strategies as he works in his writer's notebook.
- has not made a work plan with additional strategies to try in the next few days to get ready to write his draft.
- has made an unclear work plan for developing his topic before writing his draft.

CONFERENCE PURPOSE

Teach the student to make a plan for developing a seed topic before writing a draft.

MODEL TEXT

My plan or another writer's plan

◆ This conference is for students who **already** have experience developing a seed topic and are familiar with several strategies for getting ready to write in narrative and nonfiction genres (e.g., Book 1: **Topics**, *Developing a Topic* Conferences 14–28). However, up to this point, they have used these strategies **in response** to minilessons and writing conferences. This conference puts the responsibility on the students to plan their rehearsal work. Instead of teaching yet another strategy to use in their writer's notebook, teach students to draw from all they have learned about developing a seed topic to make their own work plan.

I'M GLAD YOU CAN name a couple of strategies writers use to get ready to write an op-ed. It doesn't surprise me that you know these strategies, since you have written op-eds before in writing workshop. You have learned strategies writers use to develop their seed topic in their writer's notebook.

It sounds like, as you write entries about your topic during the next few days, you are planning to use strategies as they occur to you. I'd like to show you how to do more thoughtful writing in your notebook before you draft. I want to teach you how to plan the work you're going to do to develop your seed topic.

Explain a Strategy

Most experienced writers don't just plunge into developing their seed topic and hope that they'll think of the right strategies to use as they write. Instead, before they start, they take time to think about the strategies they will use. To get ready to write in a specific genre, they decide which strategies make sense to use. They even write a formal plan for the work they're going to do.

For example, if we want to write a feature article on global warming, we make a plan to interview an expert. Or if we want to write a memoir about a parent, we may plan to spend time looking through family photo albums and watching home movies of our childhood.

This makes sense for several reasons. When we make a plan, it's more likely that we will think of the right strategies to use to develop our seed topic. And it saves time. Some strategies—getting resources, for example, or interviewing people—involve trips to the library, emails, or phone calls. If we don't plan before we start, and only think of using strategies days or even weeks later, then we might not have the time we need to get the resources or arrange the interviews.

Share Your Writing

Almost every time I start developing a seed topic of my own, I plan the strategies I'm going to use. I do this planning in my writer's notebook. I want to show you one of my plans. It is a plan for a memoir I eventually wrote about my father.

```
Plan for Dad memoir:

I need to

* dig out old photo albums
* watch home movies of dad
* reminisce with mom about him
* make a timeline of childhood memories
   of dad
* make a map of our old house — lots of
   memories attached to places in the house
   and outside in the gardens
* make a map of Tobay Beach, and
   the places we went there

Possible Mentor Text:

Cynthia Rylant's "Grandmother's Hair"
```

See how I made a list of the strategies I planned to use? For example, before I wrote even one entry in my notebook about my dad, I decided that I should look at the photo album I had from my childhood and watch some home movies of my family from when I was a kid. I thought that doing these two things would help me remember what my dad was like. Because I put these two strategies on my list, I immediately went into one of my closets at home and dug out the photo album and the home movies and used them to spark some writing about my dad. You can also see that I planned to use a bunch of other strategies, too.

As part of my planning, I also thought about which mentor text I wanted to use. You can see that I wrote down Cynthia Rylant's

Grandmother's Hair. I love the way Cynthia Rylant uses one memory about her grandmother to show something important about her own life, and I imagined writing a memoir with the same structure. It was a good thing I included this in my plan, because I couldn't find my copy of the text and had to call a friend to borrow one.

I was quite happy with the way my memoir ultimately turned out. Thinking through the strategies I wanted to use and making a clear plan for developing my seed topic before I wrote the draft got me off to a great start. Using these strategies made it possible for me to really think about my dad before I wrote my draft, and that made a huge difference in my writing.

Coach the Student

I want to help you make a work plan for developing your seed topic.

▶ Tell me your seed topic and what genre you've chosen to write in.

▶ What are some of the strategies writers use when they write in this genre? Which of these strategies do you think would be good for you to use?

▶ What mentor text could you study to help you write your draft?

Link to the Student's Writing

I'd like you to start writing your plan for developing your seed topic. I'm going to give you a list of strategies for developing a seed topic (page 155). I bet you'll get some other ideas for strategies when you look at the list for the genre you're writing in.

Remember that before writers develop a seed topic, they make a plan for the work they're going to do. Making a plan helps writers make good decisions about which strategies to use, and gives them the time they need to get resources.

◆ Many teachers have students fill out a planning sheet once they've selected their seed topic. Katie Ray discusses planning sheets in *Wondrous Words: Writers and Writing in the Elementary Classroom* (1999), as does M. Colleen Cruz in *Independent Writing: One Teacher—Thirty-Two Needs, Topics, and Plans* (2004).

SOURCES

Katie Wood Ray and M. Colleen Cruz have both described how to teach students to plan their rehearsal work before drafting in their books *Wondrous Words: Writers and Writing in the Elementary Classroom* (1999) and *Independent Writing: One Teacher—Thirty-Two Needs, Topics, and Plans* (2004).

Plan for Dad memoir:

I need to

* dig out old photo albums
* watch home movies of dad
* reminisce with mom about him
* make a timeline of childhood memories
  of dad
* make a map of our old house — lots of
  memories attached to places in the house
  and outside in the gardens
* make a map of Tobay Beach, and
  the places we went there

Possible Mentor Text:

Cynthia Rylant's "Grandmother's Hair"

© 2009 by Carl Anderson from *Strategic Writing Conferences* (Portsmouth, NH: Heinemann). This page may be reproduced for classroom use only.

Strategies for Developing a Seed Topic

PERSONAL NARRATIVE/MEMOIR

▶ Brainstorm a list of memories about the topic.

▶ Write in response to the question, "What do I want to say about this topic?"

▶ Write descriptions of important characters.

▶ Write about the main character's conflict.

▶ Write a description of the setting.

▶ Plan the structure of the written piece.

SHORT FICTION

▶ Write in response to the question, "What is my character's problem/conflict/ need?"

▶ Brainstorm a list of characteristics of the main character.

▶ Describe secondary characters and their relationships to the main character.

▶ Write (or sketch) important settings in the story.

▶ Write a short summary of the story I want to tell about the character.

▶ Plan the structure of the written piece.

FEATURE ARTICLE

▶ Brainstorm possible angles to take on the topic.

▶ Brainstorm a list of possible sections for the article.

▶ Gather information for each section (this may involve research).

▶ Make a list of resources to seek out (if needed).

▶ Plan interview questions (if needed).

▶ Plan the structure of the written piece.

© 2009 by Carl Anderson from *Strategic Writing Conferences* (Portsmouth, NH: Heinemann). This page may be reproduced for classroom use only.

Strategies for Developing a Seed Topic

OP-ED

▶ Write about my opinion, asking myself, "What exactly is my opinion about this topic?"

▶ Brainstorm reasons why I feel the way I do.

▶ Gather personal stories/anecdotes that support my reasons.

▶ Gather information to support the reasons (this may involve research).

▶ Make a list of resources to seek out (if needed).

▶ Plan interview questions (if needed).

▶ Plan the structure of the written piece.

PERSONAL ESSAY

▶ Write about my idea, asking myself, "What exactly is my idea?"

▶ Brainstorm points I want to make about the idea.

▶ Gather personal stories/anecdotes to support the points.

▶ Plan the structure of the written piece.

© 2009 by Carl Anderson from *Strategic Writing Conferences* (Portsmouth, NH: Heinemann). This page may be reproduced for classroom use only.

30

Preparing to Draft by Making a Schedule

WHAT YOU FIND

The student who could be helped by this conference has trouble managing time independently when writing a piece. She may find it difficult to:

- determine how much time each stage of the writing process will take.
- pace herself during the writing process.
- successfully meet deadlines.

CONFERENCE PURPOSE

Teach the student to independently manage her time to meet a writing deadline (imposed by someone or self-generated) by creating a schedule.

MODEL TEXT

My calendar with deadlines or another writer's calendar

◆ This conference is particularly important to have with students when they're in a unit of study in which they can choose the genre to write in. Students are usually not all in the same stage of the writing process at the same time, as they often are during a genre study, so managing time can be more of a challenge.

IT'S ALWAYS EXCITING to start developing a new seed topic, isn't it? I see that you have chosen your seed and are ready to start drafting. This is great. Before you start writing, though, there's something that I'd like to teach you about: how to make a plan to use your time to get a piece of writing done, from developing your topic all the way to publishing the finished draft. Learning how to do this is an important step for you to take toward being a truly independent writer.

When experienced writers start working on a piece of writing, they often want to complete their piece by a certain day. It may be a special occasion, like a holiday or a birthday, that they want to share the piece, or it may be a deadline for a publisher. Either way, writers don't just start writing and hope that everything will somehow get finished by the deadline. Usually, they take time to plan *on a calendar* when they're going to do all the kinds of work to get the piece done.

As writers, we try to figure out how much time it will take to develop our topic before we write a draft, how much time it will take to write a draft, and how much time to revise and edit it. And then we decide which days we will devote to that work. The result of all this planning? We are much more likely to have a finished piece by the deadline that we can share with our audience.

Share Your Writing

Whenever I start an important writing project, I think about when I want to share it with an audience. Then I get out a calendar and make a plan for how I'm going to get the piece done on time.

◆ This conference puts the responsibility *on the student* to manage their time to get a piece of writing done. Many students are used to teachers managing their time for them. This conference helps them become more independent as writers.

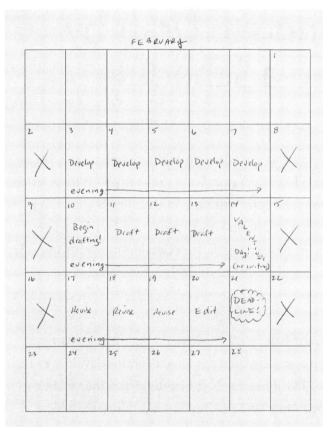

Often, I tape the calendar into my writer's notebook so that I have it with me throughout the time I'm working on the piece. Let's look together at this calendar in my notebook.

This is a plan I made for writing a memoir about my father. Since I did this piece on my own, I came up with my own deadline. I estimated that it would take me three weeks to write the memoir, so I marked on the calendar the day that was three weeks ahead. See how I've written "deadline" on this date?

Then I looked at the calendar and thought about which days I knew I *couldn't* work on the piece. Weekends aren't usually good for me as a writer, because I have two kids and like to spend time with them on the days they don't have school, so I wrote an "X" on each weekend day.

Then I had to think about how many days I was going to give each part of the writing process—developing my topic, drafting, revising, editing, publishing—so I sectioned off the calendar to give each of these stages a few days, and even wrote on each day when I thought I could get it done. This was my best guess about how much time it would take for me to move through each stage. For example, I gave myself five days to develop my topic in my writer's notebook, and I wrote down on each day that I would write in the evening after my kids would be asleep.

After I planned my time like this, I had a series of mini-deadlines to try to meet as I moved toward the big deadline. Although I don't always meet these mini-deadlines—sometimes a stage of the writing process takes me longer than I think it will or something comes up in my life and I can't write every day that I want to—having these mini-deadlines reminds me to complete each stage of the writing process. That way, I have my finished piece on time for my deadline.

Coach the Student

I'd like to help you make a plan for getting your piece done on time.

- I have a copy of a calendar for you to do this planning (page 161). What's the deadline for this piece? Mark "due" on that date.
- Are there any days that you think you won't be able to write? Why don't you put some "Xs" on those dates?
- So how many days do you think you're going to need to develop your topic before you draft?
- And when do you think you'll do this work?

Link to the Student's Writing

Now it's time for you to finish the rest of your plan on your own. Think carefully about how much time you think it might take you to move through each stage of the writing process, and record them on the calendar.

Keep in mind that experienced writers often make plans for how they're going to use time as they write a piece. Making a plan like this helps them meet their deadline.

FOLLOW-UP

Follow up on the plan that students come up with after this conference and provide feedback. Students may have made some unrealistic estimates for how long it will take them to move through the stages of the writing process. It's likely that students won't give themselves enough time for one or more stages.

If students have set their own deadline, you might suggest that they extend it further into the future—in order to have the time they need to get the writing done. As time goes by, check in with students to see how well they are keeping to their plan and if they need to revise it.

SOURCES

M. Colleen Cruz's writing about meeting deadlines in *Independent Writing: One Teacher— Thirty-Two Needs, Topics, and Plans* (2004) inspired this conference.

FEBRUARY

						1
2 ✗	3 Develop *evening* →	4 Develop	5 Develop	6 Develop	7 Develop	8 ✗
9 ✗	10 Begin drafting! *evening* →	11 Draft	12 Draft	13 Draft	14 VALENTINE's Day! (no writing)	15 ✗
16 ✗	17 Revise *evening* →	18 Revise	19 Revise	20 Edit	21 DEADLINE!	22 ✗
23	24	25	26	27	28	

© 2009 by Carl Anderson from *Strategic Writing Conferences* (Portsmouth, NH: Heinemann). This page may be reproduced for classroom use only.

© 2009 by Carl Anderson from *Strategic Writing Conferences* (Portsmouth, NH: Heinemann). This page may be reproduced for classroom use only.